LEADERSHIP AND SUCCESS

C000088591

Based on a review of the literature and several in-depth case studies, this book suggests a strategy-as-practice framework for succession and explores leadership logic, trust and followership. This book takes the reader through the key stages and disciplines required for effective top-level succession.

Corporations, growing entrepreneurial companies and family owners all must manage strong group dynamics and individual needs in a succession transition. This book includes a wide range of global client cases, including public sector organizations, corporations, entrepreneurial firms and family owners. Based on rigorous research and written in an accessible style with a focus on practical needs, readers will also be able to combine this analysis within disciplines of governance, leadership, strategy and organizational development.

This book will be of interest to students at an advanced level, academics and reflective practitioners as well as executives at the top levels of businesses.

Gry Osnes, PhD, works as an independent executive coach and researcher with family owners, entrepreneurship businesses and with chairs of boards.

Agnes Wilhelmsen, classics student, Exeter University, and research assistant for the book.

LEADERSHIP AND STRATEGIC SUCCESSION

The How and Why for Boards and CEOs

Gry Osnes and contributing author Agnes Wilhelmsen

Routledge
Taylor & Francis Group

NEW YORK AND LONDON

First published 2021
by Routledge
52 Vanderbilt Avenue, New York, NY 10017

and by Routledge
2 Park Square, Milton Park, Abingdon, Oxon OX14 4RN

Routledge is an imprint of the Taylor & Francis Group, an informa business

Library of Congress Cataloging-in-Publication Data
Names: Osnes, Gry, author. | Wilhelmsen, Agnes, author.
Title: Leadership and strategic succession: the how and why for boards and
CEOs / Gry Osnes and contributing author Agnes Wilhelmsen.
Description: Abingdon, Oxon; New York, NY: Routledge, 2021. |
Includes bibliographical references and index.
Identifiers: LCCN 2020035524 (print) | LCCN 2020035525 (ebook) |
ISBN 9780367263164 (hardback) |
ISBN 9780367685171 (paperback) | ISBN 9780429292545 (ebook)
Subjects: LCSH: Executive succession. | Leadership.
Classification: LCC HD38.2 .O86 2021 (print) |
LCC HD38.2 (ebook) | DDC 658.4/071–dc23
LC record available at https://lccn.loc.gov/2020035524
LC ebook record available at https://lccn.loc.gov/2020035525

ISBN: 978-0-367-26316-4 (hbk)
ISBN: 978-0-367-68517-1 (pbk)
ISBN: 978-0-429-29254-5 (ebk)

Typeset in Scala Sans and Joanna
by Newgen Publishing UK

For Gerd

In Memory of Lise and Arne

CONTENTS

ILLUSTRATIONS

BOXES

ABOUT GRY OSNES

Gry Osnes has 20 years of experience as consultant and executive coach, with a particular focus on leadership and succession. She is a trained psychotherapist.

Her client work is as coach for top leaders and business owners, including family owners, working with organizational design and as a developer of teams. She has written extensively on strategy, affective neuroscience and emotion, strategy formulation, succession dynamics and incubation, including for *Harvard Business Review* and other business and academic titles. She was editor of *Family Capitalism: Best Practices in Ownership and Leadership* (Routledge, 2016), which showcased best practice case studies from different types of organization in Europe, Africa, east Asia and the Americas, developed by a cross-cultural team of researchers and consultants. She has also begun a major study into the role of Boardroom Chair, so as to understand the role and associated practices for governance and top leadership.

Gry has been a pioneer of the use of affective neuroscience in coaching, convening seminars with some of the leading academics in the field. She also supervises and trains coaches in systems thinking, entrepreneurship and family ownership. Her style of working is to thrive in collaboration in teams while remaining independent in thinking.

ACKNOWLEDGEMENTS

First I want to thank all the leaders, CEOs and chairs of boards that over the years have contributed with insight into the difficulty of making succession processes successful. Many have set aside time for interviews while having very busy workdays. Also a great thanks to clients where we together have found solutions and managed different processes. Some of them allowed others and me to use their case, some openly, some anonymously, in this book. Professor Siv Boalt Boëthius and Odd Arne Tjersland, over many years, when I wrote a PhD about some of this research, were of great support and provided valuable input. Professor Leif Melin and other colleagues; Liv Hök, Jeff Jones, Jørn Skule Husemoen and Christian Selmer, have contributed, offering perspectives and insight.

I would like to thank Olive Yanli Hou for her contributions in providing in-depth, insightful coverage of business-owning Chinese families, who have been imaginative in creating alternatives to succession, and hugely enterprising in nurturing thriving business clusters. The perspectives from the Roman period and ancient Greek world built on finding sources and setting them into the context of this book. Agnes Wilhelmsen did this work in an excellent, and witty, way. Great effort has gone into editorial assistance, reviewing the latest trends in governance practices for Chapter 11 in particular, and checking out sources. Philip Whiteley has done this in an excellent and diligent way. I also want to thank Xavier Villers for the support over the years it took to gather and write up the research findings and insights from client work.

FOREWORD BY DR JULES GODDARD

There is an emerging consensus in the fields of leadership and organizational development that sees strategy formation as dynamic and constantly evolving, moving away from annual budgeting, financial targets and benchmarking. Recent findings on cognitive psychology and neuroscience lend substance to such a shift. They expose the psychological naivete of rigid command and control structures, and encourage a view of the organization which acknowledges the complex interplay of all the different constituencies. The purpose of strategy is to create customers; this is best done by being inventive and unique, not derivative or imitative, and by understanding the organization as dynamic and organic.

Few events in any organization's history illustrate the importance of such a multi-dimensional approach than the succession of a senior leader. I am therefore delighted to welcome such a valuable addition to the literature on this subject as this thoroughly researched, lucid and explanatory text by Dr Gry Osnes. It is based on 20 years of combined action research and deep academic inquiry into the actual dynamics at play when power transfers from one regime to another.

The limited – and limiting – metaphor of headhunting has tended to distort our understanding of this strategically important governing responsibility. Dr Osnes correctly stresses the importance both of addressing a multiplicity of dimensions, with an understanding that all elements are dynamic; individuals and the organization are in a constant state of flux.

The book accurately describes seven essential strategies. Visually, there is a helpful Succession Strategy Wheel for easy reference for the strategies and as an aide memoire. The author is correct to emphasize that the exercise is one of orchestration, rather than neat stages – the strategies interact with one another in unpredictable ways. One of the seven is an understanding of the uniqueness of context, and whether a succession will be used to reset, renew or radically alter organizational direction. Every organization and social setting offers cultural differences, and it is impressive that the case studies in the book are diverse, from most regions of the world, and many types of organization, from start-up to corporation, and including non-profit agencies.

She sets out how the employer, in practice usually the board, needs to prepare for a succession, and be continually aware of its succession capability. There is a helpful summary of the group and individual dynamics that can be destabilizing. This includes sensitive, at times taboo, subjects such as loss and mourning, narcissism and personal vulnerability. Throughout, the question of gender balance is given the importance it merits, and the author shows how elite preservation and groupthink have led to limited choices in succession and poor strategy execution.

Later chapters focus more on the board and the incoming leader – understanding the type of new leadership tenure that is needed and the actual handover. Examples from highly enterprising business-owning families provide insights into how incubation can be used both to reduce tension over succession to the next generation and in some cases build a thriving cluster of innovative firms.

Dr Osnes properly identifies the central duty of the board as one of care, not of strategy execution. It has a fundamental responsibility to establish and maintain trust in the organization's leadership; without it, authority collapses – and sometimes, the organization along with it. The section on the nature and importance of trust is eloquent and thoroughly researched.

The strength of the findings is bolstered by the author's eclecticism. There is impressive scholarship in combining findings from the author's own longitudinal qualitative research, those of others in an international team of researchers that she helped put together, along with a distillation of findings from strategy formulation, psychology, neuroscience, governance and family business studies. Insights from neuroscience are fully up to date, illustrating how the latest findings offer greater forensic accuracy in psychoanalytic thinking, informing us about the nature of rationality, emotions and the unconscious mind. The practical relevance is always borne in mind.

Some of the most fascinating insights come from the inspired choice of highly diverse case studies: not only conventional selections such as Alibaba today and the GE of 20 years ago, but also an African tribe, the Catholic Church, the House of Saud and Napoleon. There are some colourful examples from the ancient world: thought-provoking, entertaining and fascinating fables, supplied by a contributing author, classicist Agnes Wilhemsen.

Humans are a tribal species, and we form groups as instinctively as we breathe. For all the exotic superficial differences in human groupings, across cultures and ranging enormously in size, as members we care deeply about who is guiding them. It also matters to us whether we trust our current leaders, whether we have faith that any replacement will meet the complex set of challenges they will almost certainly inherit and whether those charged with appointing such individuals are equal to the task.

This work, which combines academic rigour with practical usefulness, will help all those involved in the succession process. The findings are contemporary and for all time.

Dr Jules Goddard,
November 2019

1

INTRODUCTION

With this book I will present analytic tools and perspectives for managing leadership successions. Readers that would find it useful are top leaders, board members, chairs of boards, family owners and advisors. I offer perspectives and insight into how complex and important succession processes are with a focus on strategy, emotions involved and group dynamics. Succession needs a strong strategic intent, while several of the dynamics are highly influenced by unconscious processes, strong individual and group emotions and cognitive biases. Understanding successions, and how authority has been constructed, is crucial for not only understanding successions in the organization but also the uniqueness of leadership in the organization. I offer an overview of the terrain and how to steer through a succession process. For the strategist and advisor, the book addresses the strategic and constructive aspects of a succession, destructive group and individual dynamics and different aspects of organizational and cultural differences.

1.1 Strategizing Complexity

From Best Practice to Complexity

A succession is an organizational event that can have a strategy process anchored in the exit and entry of a leader. At the individual level a CEO, or the chair of the board, will have their own agendas or ambitions. The latter are issues related to a leadership transition and not in itself a succession strategy. It is a role transition on the individual level with its own challenges and dynamics. Many best practice models, and planning tools, will cover these individual trajectories and they are more obvious and easy to identify. More elusive and crucial are the strategies, seven in total, individuals and groups need to carry out when attending to the challenges inherent in a succession, in order to create a successful outcome for the organization.

A best practice model or guidance of how to solve each of them will either underestimate or oversimplify the scope of the challenge. Often it reverts to a focus on individuals or sub parts of the process. The complexity is further increased since all organizations will have different degrees of maturity, historical developments, strategic challenges and specific threats that makes the consideration and outcome of each of the strategic tasks unique to the organization and time of succession. The classic dilemma of recruiting a new leader from inside or outside is just one best practice field that will be influenced by all these factors. With regards to decision makers there are governance structures such as a board, ownership group or family ownership structure that are ultimately responsible. To have a succession capability is a key part of its responsibility, that is, it should be able to trigger and manage a succession with further review and strategizing, and aligning, of these strategies.

Succession Wheel Model

There are seven succession challenges, or succession tasks, that apply to any succession process so as to bring it to a conclusion. Reviewing and addressing these seven such strategies includes, as will be described throughout, to align the outcome of each of them. Such alignment, in addition to each of them being through and executed, is what creates trust in the incoming leadership. The strategies are visually presented in the

Succession Wheel Model, which is a due diligence tool. It integrates the seven necessary succession strategies as a complete process and categorizes the complexity. They are applicable to all types of organizations. Individual or group dynamics, often also described in isolation but summarized in this book, will erode or threaten the strategizing of each of these. The model helps in identification of these threats.

Such an integrative model is also useful as guideline and planning for discussion and decision making. It is also useful for practice-based researchers. The fragmentation in approaches to understanding succession has previously led to a call for longitudinal and qualitative studies to clarify succession phenomena (e.g. Dyck et al, 2002). Complexity in understanding a succession has been a central finding from my research. The model relies on such research and offers an integrated perspective in what has been a rich but fragmented research field.

Constructive and Destructive Group Dynamics

All groups and organizations that aims to be more than a project will encounter a succession process. Successions are a group dynamic and system event that can change or reset the organization's leadership logic. When that is the case, or necessary, the succession is particularly disruptive and triggers strong dynamics. The seven strategies that optimize a succession outcome also, crucially, counteract destructive dynamics. They are linked because a succession is a constructive group dynamic that has its polarity in destructive dynamics. In some cases an undercurrent of group conflict, disagreement and individual ambitions can make a board, or owner, incapable of triggering a top leadership exit process. It is a group dynamic that ensures the organization stays alive and this is influenced by individual psychological factors. Succession is as such a stress test for the board, and succession and unconscious dynamics will also affect the board dynamics. It is one of the decisions where the board members and Chair will have an operational function. In addition to group and individual psychological processes successions are affected by institutional and cultural contexts.

The issue of responsibility to a board, or any formal governing structure, is crucial. A failed, or series of unfortunate successions, will radically erode trust in the board. Loss of trust due to a failure to trigger, or in managing and optimizing, a succession process is justified. Failed successions put the organization's very survival at risk. More typically succession is seen as a family business or family ownership issue. I will show that successions are critical for any organization and they are always complex. A non-family business can, with a good board, easily trigger and manage a succession process. However, it is harder for them to shift between, or have at the same time, a succession and an incubation process. An incubation strategy should be considered, together with a succession, as an alternative or part of a strategy for renewal. In an increasingly complex and disruptive world, both succession and incubation as process and strategy are increasingly critical for many businesses.

Ownership Evolution

Successions are crucial and are the main milestones in what I call ownership evolution. Entrepreneurial groups will, when growing and developing their business, have to address their leadership and governing systems. Family ownership and business succession; if managed by a family with robust and healthy dynamics these organizations can be resilient in crises and agile in developing new things. Each succession will reset or evolve ownership and reflect the ownership history, business and technological context and social changes such as gender diversity. In addition there are the maturation and growth of a new company or other major shifts. I use the term ownership evolution to capture the different types of ownership structures that can be used to enable, or trigger, a succession process. Again there are too many variables and conditions, including innovative solutions, to make ownership and leadership successions follow predictable patterns. Context factors, opportunities and challenges will possibly make it best to innovate and not just reset a solution from the past. Successions are also tried to be captured as predictable through using life-cycle models of businesses and/or individuals. Life stages of individuals are now less normative or predicable; we have new types of choices with regards to retirement than before, or might change careers. Other social changes on gender or the seniority of entrepreneurs also reduces what were often seen as predictable patterns.

Educative and Evocative Cases

I will use client and research cases from listed companies, state-owned companies, higher education institutions, familyowned companies, entrepreneurships and security organizations. There are cases from Asia, Middle East, Europe and the USA. More exotic cases such as religious and tribal cases are also explored for the purpose of underscoring how succession processes are influenced by institutional and cultural aspects and will have significant strategic consequences even when it is a habitual succession. The cases also underscore the evolutionary aspect of succession processes as most successions bring with them an adaptation or more radical system shift. The more radical the shift the more disruptive and complex the succession process will be. Our history is filled with such dramatic or intriguing succession stories and I have included historical cases from the classics (in boxes), written by my research assistant Agnes Wilhelmsen, to illustrate specific issues in an evocative and educational way. Famous historical events, cultural artefacts, rites and leaders will, with a succession perspective, give the reader a broader perspective on these issues.

1.2 Succession as Stress Test

For the board, succession is one of its main responsibilities, although it is not often the case that the board has much experience with succession processes. Most business leaders and board members have economic, legal, financial or other business-related experience and are therefore not trained to identify the psychological or group dynamics that arise during a succession. Yet the ability to trigger and manage a succession process is fundamental and it is often a decision the board has not been through before as a team. It is also a relatively rare event. A research project I'm currently leading has found that even the most experienced chairs of boards have at most managed three succession processes. In addition they would, at most, exited and entered a three top leadership role themselves. Even top chairs of boards who have been in charge of, or experienced as leader, four or five succession processes are wary and put substantial effort into planning and reviewing their role and the process. It is the decision-making process they are the most operationally active in. None of the succession processes they describe has been the same. One complicating factor is that a board member, CEO or chair might have roles across different types of cultures or organizations and so will engage with organizations with different types of leadership logics.

In one way or another, when I discuss successions, the underlying issues in succession processes are the struggles one has with the complexity of the process. Four aspects of a succession makes it complex: it is an emotional process, it is highly consequential for the organization, there are seven strategies necessary that need to be integrated and also counteract irrational processes and, elusively, the outcome is not only a new leader but the all-important issue of trust.

Succession is an Emotional Process

A young leader explained to me his hesitation in announcing to the board that he wanted to exit the role as follows:

> It just starts such an extraordinary push and pull all over when a succession process is triggered – the forces are extraordinary.

The leader in question had been the CEO of one of the biggest companies in the insurance sector in its country of operation since his early thirties, staying in the role for a decade. He was highly successful and could have expected several new CEO roles during his career, given that he was still only in his early 40s towards the end of a successful tenure. Yet such were the powerful forces involved, the push and pull – at board level, in his team, with employees, from the media and elsewhere in the sector – that he hesitated. The company was listed and a succession process was expected. Candidates positioned themselves for the role, while public interest and speculation grew. In addition to a leadership group resenting having a new leader they were not comfortable with, there could be implications for their ambitions and roles. Some internal members of the leadership team, as well as external candidates, were applying for the role. Appraisal of his tenure took place both in private forums, at the board level and in the media. For the board, there can be a struggle not to be drawn into a defensive position regarding miscalculation or choices made. The push and pull mentioned refers to ambitions, sense of loss, anxiety, envy and so on, of varying but often powerful intensity. Individual ambitions can dominate the process and an exiting and/or entering CEO goes through a complex set of different types of emotions. Such emotional and group dynamics constitute threats to the succession, and are important for decision makers to identify.

Successions are Highly Consequential

A succession is a strategic event that can be highly influential for the organization; more than that, it can be of crucial importance for its very survival. Its importance is most evident when a succession, or several successions in a row, have resulted in corporate collapse. A board that is passive and does not trigger a succession when needed, or recruits the wrong leader, is putting the organization at risk. A failed CEO succession can reduce confidence and the attractiveness of the role, and make further succession processes even more difficult. A series of CEO entries and premature exits can lead to a CEO revolving door, and radically reduces trust in the chair of the board and the board more generally. It can also lead to a brain-drain of key employees and leaders in addition to creating a toxic or highly anxious internal atmosphere within the organization or board.

Successions Represent Strategy Formation at Several Levels

A succession is a strategic process. It is also highly emotive and unpredictable, with powerful group dynamics that need to be acknowledged and contained. Strategic thinking is necessary to contain these, while addressing the external and internal reality of the organization. The strategies presented in this book have been shown to be effective in containing the dynamics and addressing the many different dimensions of succession. They are geared to identifying, and preparing for, the specific type of leadership necessary, as well as addressing the challenges inevitable in a succession process. Leadership effectiveness is not only about addressing strategic choices, but also about how to negotiate the role and to create a match between the leader and the development of culture, and matching these to the strategic course. A misfit between the culture of an organization and a top leader will often lead to entry difficulties and possibly a failed leadership tenure. While leadership skills and qualities are important, they are only part of the picture. It is crucial to match a leader's profile and type of drive with the most important challenges for the organization.

Succession is about Trust and Trust is Elusive

Following the succession strategies set out in this book represents an opportunity for the board to maintain or build trust between itself and its stakeholders. Stakeholders in this book are also the employees. A succession is not only triggered by a planned or unplanned exit of a CEO. It can come linked to a merger process, a big external disruption, listing or delisting of a company on the stock market or in a generational transition in a family firm. As mentioned earlier, if a board don't have a succession capability so as to trigger a necessary succession or are not successful in managing the process they will very fast lose trust.

1.3 Practical Guidance: Steering through Complex Terrain and Shaping Leadership

The strategic complexity of a succession, implication for a wider company strategy, how consequential the succession is, the emotions and group dynamics triggered, all constitute a complex terrain that this book will explore. Overall there is a focus on trust as the aggregated outcome of executing strategic succession processes, managing group dynamics and individual emotions and contextualizing succession as a process of shaping leadership. I share rich detail of in-depth action learning studies to illustrate core aspects of succession dynamics and effective practices. The insight and learning will include the following:

1. know the succession strategies necessary. Identify and define roles and key decision makers;
2. identify how different types of organizations have different logic on leadership;
3. understand the individual and group dynamics, unconscious bias and emotions;
4. be able to contextualize a succession;
5. know how to decode the unique; learn from a wide selection of cases;
6. understand how trust and succession are connected.

1.4 Research Underpinning the Book

The theory and practical approaches presented here are based on several research projects and client work. Research projects spanned several continents such as Africa, Asia, Europe and North America. Senior leaders, throughout their careers as a top executive, CEO, board member or chair of board, will have to work with or in different types of organization. There are family-owned businesses, listed companies and state-owned organizations, including a university and museum. There are also young entrepreneurial businesses.

Action Research

Action research is both a consultancy and research process where one collaborate in exploring difficult and challenging issues and problems over time and in real-life context. It is particularly useful for developing insights into how one can address new types of challenges, innovation with understanding the cognitive, emotional and strategic issues. As action researcher one can, together with the company, mutually explore what the obstacles and threats are in solving a problem. I have chosen three such cases where the research period lasted from three to ten years. The Nordic museum and university case was a study where, over ten years, I worked as the coach and advisor to the CEO from her entry to her exit. During this period I was, as action researcher, involved in several strategy processes and group facilitation projects within the organization. I was also observing the board over two years leading up to the CEO's exit. Another such action research project was the Ottolenghi case, a restaurant and retail business based in London, where I worked for four years, initially as the CEO's coach, helping a group of founders and owners to develop the governing function of their business so that it would have a succession capability. A third case was a publicly listed company where I was an advisor for a female chair of board and helped her carve out the role while addressing a succession process.

In-depth Multi-case Studies

Over some years a team of researchers I led explored family ownership cases from different parts of the world. We had family-owned business cases from China, Sweden, the USA, Israel, Germany, the UK, Tanzania and Columbia. Some of this material will be used to illustrate many aspects of succession in this book. Family businesses constitute a major part of all economies. A family business, at least in the way succession has traditionally been practised, faces a more complex succession challenge emotionally. While this has always been the case, certain social trends are changing family ownership and leadership, and practices are being altered accordingly. The younger generations are, to a greater degree, seeking business education, and this includes sisters and daughters who are now being included into active ownership and leadership roles, where previously the businesses would have been patriarchal. Other research, in addition to mine, shows that successions in family businesses are changing and making these types of organizations more competitive. Imaginative alternatives to a conventional handover of an existing businesses, for example through new entrepreneurship, are being developed.

Interview Research on the Role of Chair of the Board

Over a period of two years a research team that I have led has interviewed chairs of boards in Scandinavia, Europe, the UK and the USA. It was ongoing at the time of writing, with 60 chairs interviewed. One of our topics was the management and challenges of CEO succession. While the results from this research project are not presented in full in this book, there were some major insights from very experienced chairs that will be used to illustrate important lessons and challenges. The chairs are mainly in role at companies that are listed on the stock market. But to our surprise, at least in the smaller Scandinavian countries, many chairs had a wide experience in different types of boards such as listed companies, big family businesses and in smaller entrepreneurial firms. Such diversity in exposure to different types of organizations made these interviews particularly interesting and insightful.

1.5 Organization of the Book

The book is divided in two parts. Part I covers the work and preparation that a board or top leaders need to do so as to be able to oversee the exit of a leader and selection of a new one. Part II talks about the succession process from the perspective of handing over and authorizing a new CEO. These two processes – the exit and entry of a CEO – are linked but for clarity on main issues they are dealt with in two separate parts. This also makes it easier to show how the planning process of exiting a CEO and recruiting a new one entails the preparation for the actual handover of the role.

Part I: Exit of a CEO and Strategic Successions

Chapter 2 describes the birth of a governance structure in young ventures, illustrated by the Ottolenghi case. Also covered are new practices in family ownership and their leadership, corporate succession and inside/outside succession processes. The much-lauded succession at General Electric at the turn of the century is featured. There is also discussion on renewal, a transitional approach to succession.

Chapter 3 presents seven necessary succession strategies: resetting or renewing authority; the creation of a mandate as objectifying and making explicit the expectation for future leadership; the creation of a wish list of leadership skills; defining the succession pool; defining executive authority; the deal; and the hand-over. Each of them has at some time been conflated with succession planning in the round, and almost always to the expense of other disciplines. Some of these strategies have been ignored completely during the succession process, despite their significance.

Chapter 4 goes into depth on group dynamics as a source of destructive succession processes, or neglect of key disciplines. Most practitioners will acknowledge the affects and emotions triggering, or being triggered by, a succession, but the group dynamics are more elusive, more difficult to acknowledge and identify. I describe several critical group dynamics that can threaten to unravel a succession. While a board and top leadership team can with more ease identify individual emotions or affects, they will themselves be easily drawn into these group dynamics. Several cases are used to describe each of them. The most significant group dynamics in the context of succession are groupthink, scapegoating, over-idealization or marginalization of a leader and elite preservation.

Chapter 5 explores the individual emotions and affects that a successor can trigger in the exiting leader, among board members and employees. They can be expressed within, or even be the trigger of establishing, hidden corridors of power. In healthy organizations and with a mature board they are acknowledged and addressed so that they don't determine the succession outcome. The emotions addressed are: loss of safety, mourning, rage and rivalry, fragility and vulnerability as the basis for hubris.

Chapter 6 is titled "Focus on leadership logics" and will go into depth in several different types of organizations and show how different logics on leadership affect the succession process. The institutional logic will change according to the type of institution and in this chapter four unusual succession and leadership systems are explored: The Norwegian "Oil Fund" (Norwegian Bank Investment Fund), The Vatican, the Saudi Arabian Royal Family succession and Mossad, an Israeli security organization.

Part II: Entry of a CEO and Followership

Chapter 7 is about the entry of a new leader and the expectation established upon arrival. Is the new CEO an agent of evolution or transformation? Every succession involves at least some change, but there is invariably a balance to be struck between continuity and evolution or radical shift. It is usually assumed that an external candidate is needed for significant change, however it is not proven that this is always the case. I discuss how the decision in 2019 of the major bank HSBC to open up the CEO role to outsiders was significant.

Chapter 8 explores the handover and CEO entry into the new role. It builds on Chapter 7, but explores more technical aspects. Sequencing of the different transitions is important. To achieve a favourable transition atmosphere, a delicate dance in establishing initial followership occurs. The incumbent-successor dynamics are sensitive, and can involve rivalry or mistrust. I use a knowledge organization, a university and museum in Europe, as an example.

Chapter 9 explores ownership evolution and unique features of succession options and dynamics in family ownership. I use some highly successful cases to show how families can use either succession or incubation, or a mixture of the two, in handing over assets and opportunities to the next generation. Incubation includes serial entrepreneurship, new venture and cluster ownership. This chapter also discusses the importance of values and culture shaping the leadership logic. Case studies include the entrepreneurial FOTILE Chinese company and an Israeli tourism firm.

Chapter 10 seeks to understand how authority and the granting of executive power, are often overlooked but can be sources of tension or conflict within the succession process. There are differences between Europe and the USA in terms of board structure and the authorizing process, but the practice in the USA of combining CEO and chair of board roles is in decline. A lame duck period while an exiting leader is serving out a notice period may require sensitive handling. The Chinese retail giant Alibaba case is used to illustrate future trajectories on executive discretion, power and authority.

Chapter 11 illustrates how a succession is an ultimate stress test for a board. Whereas many of the cases in the book illustrate positive outcomes, this chapter features an example where abuse of privilege led to a collapse of trust in one organization, and how an established career path of CEO-to-chair can be a warning sign. It includes a quote from the chair who oversaw a successful turnaround. The board does not have an executive function; its ultimate duty is one of care.

Chapter 12 discusses social and psychodynamic aspects in a succession. Some concepts were introduced in Chapters 4 and 5 on group and individual dynamics. This chapter delves more deeply into such issues, drawing on the latest findings from neuroscience and psychology. Aspects covered include: affects and feelings – they are never absent; loss and mourning; entitlement and rage; rivalry; narcissism; and followership.

Reference

Dyck, B., Mauws, M., Starke, F. A., & Mischke, G. A. (2002). Passing the baton: The importance of sequence, timing, technique and communication in executive succession. *Journal of Business Venturing*, 17(2), 143–162.

PART I

EXIT OF A CEO AND STRATEGIC SUCCESSION

2

SUCCESSIONS AS CROSSROADS

A succession is a set of events and processes happening over time. Employees and stakeholders can often become preoccupied with the succession and it shows how they share often incomplete information, gossip and speculation. It can also look to the past with stories of former CEO's exit and entry processes and how they influenced the history of the company. Somehow it resonates with anyone with a stake in the organization; employees, shareholders, local communities. In addition to normal curiosity the extra attention successions get is due to one key factor: trust. It is a theme throughout the book; distrust, and the establishment or maintenance of trust, are involved in all the processes around successions. As such, succession events trigger curiosity and engagement from employees and stakeholders in informal information sharing and/or speculation. Such gossip and information exchange, and speculation, are ways to try deciphering if the process and a new leader can be trusted.

Over the history of an organization, the top leadership role will evolve, sometimes in abrupt ways to due to external changes or change in ownership, sometimes due to internal crises. Exploring the history of top leadership roles, such as the CEO and chair of the board, reveals the pressure points and shifts. Each succession can therefore have a unique historical context. Some successions are habitual in nature, resetting what is seen as legitimate. Other contexts can create radical shifts, and these are prone to trigger more disruption. During the evolution of an organization, the institution format and assumptions may be going through radical change. It can be a case of a founder group being bought by private equity, a listed company becoming privately owned or a state-owned company being privatized. In such succession processes the logic about what is seen as legitimate leadership often changes.

Whether there is a slow evolution, or a radical shift in how the top leadership role(s) are made legitimate, there are different leadership logics that are shifting. Our political institutions, state, religious and educational organizations, have gone through such changes. I will not explore political successions in great depth, but I use some examples to point out how they are, even in their ancient forms, a reference point in how we refer to authority.

In most Western countries succession of the most senior executive positions is now determined by elections. Democratic institutions developed from other types of governance structures such as kingdoms and/or tribal structures, which typically had different types of succession processes. Old succession systems, now evolved into new systems, were linked to the ownership of land; succession was the birth right of the eldest son of the principal owner of strategic assets. Land succession could be disrupted by the intervention of a ruler. Religious organizations, such as churches or monasteries, also used to own land, and many still do. Yet through all the modernizing changes, succession loses none of its interest, importance and potential for drama. It provides subject matter for academic inquiry in different fields, including history, political science, social anthropology, psychology and sociology.

During the research for this book we witnessed a high-profile democratic succession that took place in the USA, giving us the example of presidents as starkly different as Barack Obama and Donald Trump following one another. In the USA, the tension between the executive and legislative authority creates tension in a country that simultaneously grants its president strong executive authority, incorporating the post of Commander in Chief, yet insists that the individual is equal before the law, subject to the risk of impeachment proceedings. In 2000 the election result was so close between candidates George W. Bush and Al Gore that for some days uncertainty lay over the succession and the result was determined by the Supreme Court. Despite these modern institutions we still have old authority, with different succession systems and legitimacy, as metaphors or reference points to how we talk and think about authority. Box 2.1 shows a moment. with its complex context, that captures different and contrasting notions of authority.

BOX 2.1 QUEEN ELIZABETH AT A CROSSROAD

By Agnes Wilhelmsen

Below we see Queen Elizabeth II of the United Kingdom and President Kwame Nkumrah of Ghana photographed dancing at a farewell ball in Accra, the country's capital, in 1961. Tensions were growing in the period leading up to the Queen's visit. Bombs had gone off in Accra just days earlier. Ghana had only recently gained its independence from Britain, in 1957 under President Nkumrah, and fears emerged as to the Queen's visit potentially undermining Ghana's freedom from colonial rule. The Queen, against advice from both Parliament and the former Prime Minister Churchill, defiantly made the visit. Reportedly she was mindful of the emerging closeness between the Ghanaian President and the Soviet Union, which in turn would spark fears as to Ghana's potential departure from the Commonwealth, the alliance of democratic nations that succeeded the British Empire. This picture rather glamorously encapsulates an iconic moment of commitment for the two nations and for the Commonwealth.

Several types of leadership, and succession, are captured in the image and the context. Ghana, in common with most of sub-Saharan Africa, was traditionally governed by tribal structures that have often had different succession systems than European monarchies. Most of them were patriarchal but some were dominated by the female line of succession. They were linked to stewardship, rather than ownership, of land. Further, Ghana had become independent, with a democracy rather than tribal rule, and a sovereign nation state.

The picture also alludes to tension between the monarchical authority and the elected representative government in England. Queen Elizabeth's own succession is in itself an interesting event, a crossroad between the past and the future. She took on the role as ruling monarch immediately after the death of King George VI in 1952. Initially Elizabeth had not expected to assume the throne. Her father King George VI was not in line for the throne until Edward VIII's scandalous abdication in 1936 following his choice to marry the divorcee Wallis Simpson, which the Church of England regarded as morally unacceptable. Despite Elizabeth being maneuvered into this role as Queen she now holds the record as the longest reigning monarch in history.

Source: *Alamy*

While Europe has had a long tradition with monarchies, those that still exist today hold mostly symbolic power, yet still the notions of King, Queen or Chief retain a strong allusion to authority or reverence. In tribal succession, while the oldest male son is often expected to inherit the title, this has not been universal practice, even in long-established regimes. In some tribes the land was held collectively and female and male members had complementary rights. The role of the tribe chief would be to settle any land disputes. In countries like Zimbabwe, women owned the produce they had from agriculture, while men took care of cattle. With colonization, many collectively owned land arrangements within tribes were converted into private ownership by the colonizing power. Some land would be then owned by a chief, while other pieces of land were allotted to settlers. After independence from colonial powers, new political institutions, aiming for democracy, came into being. This ushered in a long period of turbulence and reform, in which the issue of land ownership became highly political and contentious.

In the United Kingdom the Parliament changed the law pertaining to monarchic succession in 2015. The oldest male child was normally the successor even if they had an older sister. Now the law changes this custom so that it is the oldest child regardless of gender, who will be successor to the throne. Such equality with respect to gender has been in place in the monarchies in Sweden and Norway for about 50 years.

I will in this chapter show how succession as a process can radically change an organization and use three different cases that show how succession themes and processes trigger, and are a part of, organizational evolution. Most advisors, coaches and chairs of boards will, at some time in their career, encounter a major organizational change with implications for leadership and succession. This may be a new venture, a family changing the governing structure or leadership in a generational transition, or a major and complex new leadership system replacing the senior executive. In other succession cases the organizational change is more one of evolution, although this still has implications for succession. The cases presented in this chapter are three classical succession processes that practitioners encounter.

2.1 Ottolenghi and New Entrepreneurship

I have to balance the level of structure and fluidity – this makes us able to innovate continuously.

Yotam Ottolenghi

Ottolenghi is a restaurant and retail business based in London, founded by the Israeli-British chef Yotam Ottolenghi and two partners in 2002. The founding team comprised two chefs and a business manager, running a small restaurant/delicatessen that focused on food innovation, serving a mixture of Middle East and Italian cooking.

The group of three founders, with the Managing Director (MD) as one of the first employees, began operating as a small group with informal leadership roles, as there were just ten employees. During the first 12 years it had grown into a business with four more restaurants and a publishing outlet producing recipe books. They ended up having 250 employees and as the business grew, the top leadership role, the MD, had to scale up and develop a more strategic role. Fourteen years after its launch, the founding group, including the MD, went through yet another transition at which accountability, from the MD's perspective, became an issue. By this stage the business had 350 employees. What was then an informal leadership system had no defined formal board.

By this stage they were running several companies as the publishing business had grown and was owned principally by one of the founders. With an increase of different brands and new types of ventures, there was a need for some type of governing structure. The MD role was changed to a CEO role and the leader of a leadership team, rather than a member of an informal founder and leadership team. The shift to CEO status clarified her role, gave it a clear strategic scope, and she would be reporting to a board. In that sense the business, and its top structure, would have a succession capability. They would be able to trigger a succession and she would be accountable, but also have a firm grip on the leadership of the main business. The board comprised a new chair, a minority owner and another external member. Nearly 20 years after the founding of the business the group would start discussions about developing an ownership forum that only had the main shareholders as members. Ownership forums, in family and non-family entrepreneurial businesses, often define the 10–15 year plan for the owners. This covers strategic questions such as whether they will have several companies, and also set out financial parameters connected to the ownership. It further instructs the board in what it is to achieve for the owner(s).

The case illustrates how developing a board that has a succession capability can be a critical feature of a relatively young company. It is a typical development when ventures are able to professionalize their business and grow. In this case none of the founders or leaders left the company during the process. During such processes, all involved will have significant changes to their roles and this is why they can take some time. Founders, shareholders and leaders might have over a long time period developed roles based on complementary skills and informal agreements. A deep sense of identification with the role leads to changes being felt as a threat and they can be upsetting. Informal groups can feel safe and comfortable; one is secure in the role, as one has been in the past, if it is supported by good relationships. Only when the strategic risk, and emotional turmoil or pain that comes with conflicts, become too troubling are ventures willing to add some structure. In hindsight, once effective structures are in place, leaders appreciate the outcomes and there is less time taken up by conflict. The business develops a stronger identity for everyone, including employees, that relies less on individuals. A succession capability and accountability bring with it a narrative that the future will be taken care of. Such evolution is crucial for ventures to succeed, and at the core of how new ventures maintain their role of contributing to growth in the economy. As the CEO reflects on the development:

> Well, you know, it was very hard at times. All of us who were here when we started had left our homeland, somehow escaping for different reasons, and we were a very tight group and very close friends – like a family.
>
> And we still are – but it has been a roller coaster. I was sometimes worried that we would not be able to save the friendship or the business – or both. But with some time and a step-by-step approach we got a better grasp of the roles we had and got a board. Now there is a better distinction between friendship and the decision-making process. We have an excellent board member who is from the outside, and not a member of our friendship group. We are still innovative and talk about ideas, but we don't take decision unless it is in the role as leader or at the board.

Importantly, in Ottolenghi the reforms were driven by the CEO herself as she sought to have a role where accountability and responsibilities were clear. While she had worked with the founders almost from the beginning, her role had changed from being the leader of 10 employees to 350. As is typical for such businesses, the founders and key employees and leaders had developed strong friendships and emotional ties. With informal and unclear roles one had a sense of being innovative, but often a lack of clarity creates conflicts that hinder the innovation. With the right structures, innovative capacity can be organized and improved.

Objections from founders to overly formal processes may be valid. There needs to be a balance between formality of systems, including a succession capability, and adaptability. This point of a company's development is often the entry point, or trigger, for the company to seek an outsider to help. Understanding the human dimension, while also working so as to find a good enough system of accountability between the owners and the top leaders, are crucial tasks in such work. This maturation involves a notion of seeing governance, accountability and succession capability as a process that takes time and is a part of the evolution of the organization. It is necessary to balance a sense of urgency with the patience necessary for the key individuals, such as a CEO, to develop into the roles.

Ventures less successful than Ottolenghi in creating top leader accountability and governing structures often become burdened with conflicts among founders and employees/leaders. Another risk is to be in a strategic drift where a consistent discussion, formulation and execution of strategy is not taking place. Selling the business is often a default option. A crossroads for entrepreneurial firms such as Ottolenghi is the point at which leaders need to determine, after they are successful with a more professional leadership of their business(es), what the long-term future is. Shall it become a family business or a broader partnership? It could be sold and the capital generated incorporated into a portfolio run by a family office who invest in new ventures. Alternatively, it could be bought by a bigger, possible publicly listed company, and be assimilated into a multi-brand corporation. From the initial founder experience, as long ago as 20–30 years earlier, the lives of all key personnel – founders, key leaders, long-serving staff – are intertwined and affected by the changes in the business and how it evolves.

2.2 New Practices in Family Leadership: Shipping

Succession in family-owned businesses is often viewed from the outside, and in the public realm, as a zero sum game: the eldest son wins the sole prize of leading executive role in the sole family business. The others lose, accepting consolation prizes. Yet this is an artificially narrow choice, and limited framing of the choices available. In the following case I will show how social changes around gender, possibly also a hidden story about women in strong informal roles, led to a generational transmission became a crossroad where innovative leadership structure was created. A big family-owned shipping company, based in northern Europe, was controlled by the fourth generation at the time of writing, having been founded in the early 20th century. It had developed a strong business, with a high reputation for design excellence and technical innovation. At the time of writing, the leadership consisted of two siblings, a sister as CEO and a brother as vice-CEO. Regional regulations would demand they had a board and most board members were external. The three siblings of the fourth generation, as owners, gave strategic direction to the board and at the same time the siblings would report to the board. Another sister had, in a collaboration with them, built a property company where they allocated revenue from the main business. In this way were they able to direct dividends and counteract the high risk involved in their main business with investment in less risky assets. A long-term plan was that the property business would develop into a family office for their children, the fifth generation.

It began in a local and modest way, like most firms, but expanded rapidly as the founder, a mechanical engineer, and his wife saw the opportunities as shipbuilding switched from wooden sail-powered to steel-constructed motorized vessels. It had become a global and successful business by the 21st century. There was a tradition of female leadership, despite this being a male-dominated industry. In the second generation, the male head of the business died suddenly and his wife, grandmother to the current owning generation, took over the business before handing it on to her son. In keeping with many of the cases studied as part of the research for this book, women took on significant roles and influenced the way leadership is organized in the business. In the case of this shipping firm, where the fourth generation daughter assumed the CEO role, this inclusive succession system built on an existing tradition. She had a background in marketing, sales and PR, while her brother the vice-CEO had an engineering background.

Decisions are reached by consensus, with the siblings carving out agreements even though it may appear to be a hierarchy to the outside world. The consensus follows robust and open debate within the family, bolstered by ties of trust and a commitment to cooperation. Conflict of opinion is accepted and tolerated, and often used to generate debate that results in new innovative ideas. Obviously such a fair-minded and honest decision-making process is most likely to take place in a family with a cooperative culture, where egos are tempered. The third generation leader, their father, had educated his four children in such a democratic fashion, emphasizing equality. Distributed leadership, including a leading role for women, is historically not new in family businesses, but it has been to some extent hidden, as laws have sometimes made ownership or inheritance impossible or difficult for women. Such a distribution of power, and increasing roles for women as owners and leaders, seems to be a general trend in family businesses. Rather than a single top leader and associated concentration of power, several senior leadership roles are created, suited to the abilities and temperament of each. In this business a board with an external chair and external board members was useful in separating the family's ownership roles. The family as a group instructed the board, while in their leadership roles they were accountable to the board. The board would also be important in resolving unresolved disputes on strategy in the business that the siblings would respect.

2.3 Corporate Dilemma in General Electric

In a globalized economic world, with huge corporate behemoths, new sources of non-democratic power have emerged. It is sometimes not clear which jurisdiction they are based in, and to which they should pay taxes. Size and complexity also make them impossible for outsiders to understand, even though they are reviewed by investors and a stock market, and even though shareholders would be expected to react to bad practices or lack of transparency. In the 20th century the stock markets in New York and London responded to the increasing size and complexity of corporations and, with some differences, imposed some regulations on these "kingdoms".

When it came to succession, due to the complexity it was generally seen as difficult, if not impossible, for a top leader to come in from the outside. Pride was also invested in the organization's capability to generate their own top leaders. An example of a corporate succession much lauded at the time, but with relatively disappointing long-term outcomes, was that at the USA giant conglomerate GE in the early 21st Century. For 20 years Jack Welch was the all-powerful Chairman and CEO of GE, feted as one of the greatest executives of his generation in numerous adulatory media profiles. He transformed an industrial powerhouse into what was effectively a conglomerate, including financial services and media. He had increased market value from $12 billion to $410 billion during his tenure. In 1999, Fortune magazine declared him to be the finest executive of the 20th Century. Welch himself was more modest, remarking that his true success would be judged by the performance of the company over the following 20 years. At the time of writing, that period has passed, and the verdict is less than stellar.

Welch's anointed successor Jeff Immelt left in 2017, after being forced out by activist investors. The market valuation had approximately halved, and his successor had reversed one of Welch's acquisitions, GE Capital, and divested the media group NBC Universal. Welch's philosophy – that with the best management a conglomerate can succeed in any sector if it is the number 1 or number 2 – was no longer viable. Even compared with other conglomerates, such as Honeywell, GE had not performed well in relative terms, losing around a quarter of market value in the decade to 2017, compared with a more than doubling of Honeywell's value (Stewart, 2017).

At the time of the handover, in 2000–2001, the succession process was celebrated as a model of its kind, focusing on the individual talent of the future leader: the talent pool, the identified candidate and the handover, as an article in the Los Angeles Times shows. The need for strategic continuity was taken for granted. One excerpt read:

> For the better part of a decade ... Welch has been intensely focused on determining and preparing his successor, saying in a 1991 speech: "From now on, [choosing my successor] is the most important decision I'll make. It occupies a considerable amount of thought almost every day."
>
> (Girion, 2000)

Preparations for Jack Welch's successor had begun a full decade before his retirement. He gave priority to development of senior managerial capability at the company. There followed the creation of a talent pool; drawing up of a shortlist and meritocratic approach to identify the best candidate; defining the mandate and meticulous planning of the handover.

There are many mitigating factors for Jeff Immelt's apparently less successful tenure. To begin with, the sheer hype surrounding Jack Welch at the time of his exit, and his anointment of a successor, almost certainly meant that GE stock had been overvalued. After taking over, Immelt had to confront the aftermath of the 9/11 attacks, the dotcom crash and the financial crash that followed seven years later. Also, the activist investors who forced Jeff Immelt's departure were aggressively pushing a short-term agenda of raising debt and releasing cash to shareholders, cutting some investments (Stewart, 2017). At the time of writing, it was not clear that this would be a better strategy.

The hype surrounding Welch hid weaknesses in the corporate structure: its complexity and the high contribution of financial services – something which was later exposed by the financial crash. It could be argued that the principal weaknesses at GE lay in complacency surrounding the business model and strategy developed under Jack Welch. With such a revered leader as Welch personally overseeing the preparation of three candidates, and determining his own successor, this can be seen with hindsight as a process that led to passivity of the board. At the time of the succession, in 2000–2001, the strategy that appeared obvious to the GE board was one of continuity, and the succession pool was selected accordingly. There was a mismatch between the apparent emphasis in 2000–2001 on continuity, and the marked strategic change under the successor. As such a legacy seems to have stifled shifting from one area to a new and change was forced by events. A possible crossroad was not envisioned by the board. Immelt received criticism not for selling NBC Universal and GE Capital, but for not doing so sooner, as he reduced diversification at the conglomerate (Stewart, 2017).

2.4 A Transitional Approach

The board needs to create time and space to use a succession as a renewal opportunity. A succession is a transition that is a strategic space and it has the potential to be filled with discussions and thoughts that are unexpected and surprising. This can trigger conflict, provocation and innovative ideas. It further has the potential to enable leaders to explore and analyse the external context and the organization, so as to ground the decision in a complex reality. Transitions such as a succession have the best outcomes when they have a strong reality orientation, but are combined with innovation and playfulness. Renewal builds on such transitional capacity; not only for start-ups, but for any organization requiring renewal, adaptation or change. It also demands, and develops, an intellectual and an emotional capacity (Osnes, 2016). Human groups, of any kind, become stagnant if they do not create opportunities for exploration and innovation. Findings from different disciplines, chiefly psychoanalysis and neuroscience, now converge to support such transitional approaches. The importance to human development of play has only recently been more fully explained. Affective neuroscience now has confirmed observations from Winnicott, a pioneering psychoanalytic researcher, that playfulness is hard-wired in the brain and together with curiosity, another hard-wired drive, is the source for renewal. Another psychoanalyst, John Bowlby, wrote about attachment to people or objects so as to feel safe. A radical change can trigger a loss and needing to feel safe, and to mourn, is equally hard-wired in the brain.

Processes of renewal and loss, and emotions they relate to, are, as I will show throughout, important in succession.

Framing the strategic potential and implications of succession should include some historical perspectives. It can be a historical event for the organization with changes in the economic, sector or political context that lead to bigger or smaller transitions and the evolvement of the organization. Within this already complex picture there are the context of the individual leaders as well as the leaders on the board. The art of handling succession is to align the interests, motivation, abilities and needs of the individual and the institution at crucial periods in the respective historical trajectories. In a disruptive succession, where the organization goes through what for the organization is a historical change, the emotions and group dynamics will be extra strong and possibly destructive. At this point, as in a normal succession, one needs to go in deep: to understand the emotions and drives, the exit and entry processes, what happens to the group and the strategies for the business. Hence seven specific succession strategies are suggested in this book (see Chapter 3). As a process of transition, succession is an opportunity for an organization to adapt and renew itself (Amado, 2005).

Practice Summary

While other chapters emphasize the importance of different dimensions of the succession process – the strategy, the culture, the collective and the individual – this needs to be overlaid on an understanding of how these interactions are in continual flux through time. For a practitioner trying to enter, maybe without knowing the organization well, into the complexity of successions and the evolution or shift a succession often implies, a focus on the role history is a good entry point. Rather than the general story of organizations, the history of the CEO role, the chair role, and other key roles such as founders and active owners, will in a more precise way show the implications of governance changes, political events, individuals' influence, strategic decisions, etc. This approach also allows for taking into account and recording unusual events that otherwise would not have been predicted. It will reveal the smaller steps that are required to adapt and evolve, or show that more radical changes are necessary. Overall it gives a historical context for an upcoming succession and how legitimacy has been created, and how it will be created again. Individual leaders may have been significantly influenced by the roles they have held, or be more neutral. Such individual narratives are often gossiped about, and are a part of the history, but they may not be the central arc of the organizational narrative with regards to upcoming successions.

In this regard, this book will have a bias toward the European style of governance with a separate chair of the board and CEO. I later show in Chapters 9, 10 and 11, how this practice is increasingly used in the USA. This is also advocated for family-owned businesses. In the evolution of young ventures formalizing leadership teams, boards and ownership structures, these steps are necessary but take time and need to be done in a step-by-step manner. In my consultancy experience, and from interviews with board members, a smooth and unrushed transition from an informally managed venture to a business with a leadership team and board can take from one and a half to two years. The same is often the case with family businesses, although these often have more urgency in establishing an ownership forum.

References

Amado, G., & Vansina, L. (Eds.). (2005). *The transitional approach in action*. Karnac Books.

Girion, L. (2000, December 3). GE succession a leadership lesson, *Los Angeles Times*. www.latimes.com/archives/la-xpm-2000-dec-03-wp-60548-story. html

Osnes, G. (2016). *Family capitalism: Best practices in ownership and leadership*. Routledge.

Stewart, J. B. (2017, 15 June). Did the Jack Welch model sow seeds of GE's decline? *New York Times*. www.nytimes.com/2017/06/15/business/ge-jack-welch-immelt.html

Winnicott, D. W. (2012). *Playing and reality*. Routledge.

3

STRATEGIC SUCCESSIONS

Most top leaders, owners, boards and chairs have stories and experiences to share on successions. Both my client work and research on succession processes are rich in detail. The topic is high on the agenda of what top executives find challenging. The chairs of boards, or owners, I have interviewed or worked with have often only been involved in, or in charge of, one CEO succession process as board member or former CEO. The most experienced chairs have been involved with three to five CEO succession processes, rarely more. Even very experienced board members and top leaders express a strong wish for understanding of the dynamics of succession. The origin for this is that there are several levels of understanding necessary. Even with a strong focus on the right procedure and careful steps in the execution there are always surprises and no two successions are the same. A chair, board or owner has to review if the guidelines in place are relevant or will have to adapt to new realities. The step is to review the procedure and succession system. It is important one agrees to this and doesn't automatically reset it as it is the first strategy in a succession. An unexposed tension or disagreement will make addressing the other six strategy challenges difficult if not impossible. This is, for experienced leaders, less complex than the human side of successions, which include group and individual dynamics. These group dynamics and individual emotions that successions can trigger are not only about what others do but what they themselves will be a part of. A high degree of independent thinking, reviewing one's role and action in the course of the process, and self-reflection are necessary.

Employees and other stakeholders will monitor the process, and if there are some missteps they will suddenly pay close attention and start to scrutinize the process. Why this scrutiny and focus? The elusivity of trust and the potential for dire consequences of faulty or sloppy judgements are at the core of this scrutiny. An owner or chair has to create trust while recruiting a leader that, depending on the organization's situation, can be critical for the future of the organization. Not all successions are crucial for what can be the continuation of the success of the organization. A new leader can immediately destroy a successful trajectory if too ego driven, or too driven to make a difference rather than addressing what the needs of the organization are. The way one defines the expectation for the next leadership tenure is one of the succession strategies that creates leadership, second to having the right procedure in place. The crucial complexity emphasized here is that a strategy approach includes how individual and group dynamics erode strategic decision making and the trust given to the process and outcome. The overall effect is a reduction in trust in the process and the leader. The complexity and sensitivity are two of the reasons one most often seeks to keep the process secret while one has to address an increased interest and need for information so as to create trust. There are several good reasons for such secrecy. Some candidates would not come forward if it were known they were seeking a new job. They might already have a top leadership role somewhere else. This complicates the communication decision makers can have around the process.

It will be discussed in some depth in the next two chapters, 4 and 5, how highly emotional and irrational successions can become. Perhaps more than any other strategic process for the organization, second only to a merger or major staff reductions, it is a process that creates a lot of emotion. An additional reason for secrecy is that it is a complex strategic process that can only with difficulty be clearly communicated during the process. Based on my own and others' research, client cases where I have been involved with the organization or owner for years, this chapter describes seven succession strategies and a Succession Strategy Wheel. It is an overarching and practice-based model for succession planning. It has usefulness on several levels:

- it captures the strategies necessary for creating a successful succession process;
- these strategies are distinctly different but linked and erosion of one of them, will have implications for the others;
- specific emotions and group dynamics will erode the different strategies and these can be identified in the process or in a due diligence review;
- it eases the communication, without reaching details, so as to explain the process and outcome.

3.1 Preparation and the CEO Exit as the Triumph

Before describing the succession process as a system and organizational event I will address, and return to throughout, the individual dimension, which is so often the initial thought or association many have about successions. Many stories in the public realm, such as in plays and films, focus on the story of the individual and have heroic or failed leaders. While individual leaders are a part of the succession process, obviously, they are in their own trajectory of career and life plan events and ambitions. The organization, and a succession, is in the trajectory of the organization and its survival. For many career-focused individuals, achieving performance targets as a CEO is often presented, in the business press and business education, as the ultimate career goal, while for some simply becoming the CEO is the target. At the personal level we all tell ourselves stories about how we are doing. A career involves expectations, of oneself as well as from others, and this all forms part of such a narrative. Becoming a CEO is often a long-awaited goal, and those who achieve it have spent considerable effort, both emotionally and intellectually, in reaching such a highly prized goal. Importantly, others will notice and one receives congratulations. As such the process can feel triumphal. It is therefore paradoxical to think that the triumph will be on the exit from the role. A real leadership triumph, as metaphor for success, is another type of achievement – completing a tenure successfully. In the history of the Roman Triumph, where the term triumph originates from, there were different practices to guard against hubris. For the ones with an interest in history, and how our current society and civilization has developed, the ritual and original meaning of "a triumph" is described in Box 3.1. It captures how the Roman Empire, in different ways over its history, would at a system and symbolic level acknowledge and try to symbolize the essence of victory and the importance of humility.

BOX 3.1 THE ROMAN TRIUMPH

By Agnes Wilhelmsen

The Roman triumph was an elaborate procession and a thrilling demonstration of conquest. It was reserved for victorious generals (consuls, praetors or dictators were the only offices that legally command an army – *imperium*). It was awarded if the general had achieved an outstanding victory or expanded the empire, which shows how the Roman triumph intended to underline the Roman Republic's commitment to meritocracy (Beard, 2009). Strictly speaking the Roman triumph was a civil ceremony and religious rite, an occasion most likely based on Etruscan and Greek culture linking the *vir triumphalis* (man of triumph) to a king, even a deity. This *vir triumphalis* was the centre of the extravagant ceremony, he would be riding a chariot, clad in a purple and gold toga. There would be the regalia associated with Roman monarchy and the Statue of Jupiter Capitolinus, and his face would be painted red.

All these accessories encapsulate an air of divine authority as well as kingship. The general Roman attitude towards kings is negative, the last of whom being Tarquinius Superbus, an unpopular king who was overthrown and exiled in 509 BCE. The trappings of monarchy could receive an ambiguous response under the Roman Republic; nevertheless, the parade was a spectacular event. The spoils and captives of the general would be in front and his army following behind. The abundance of the plunder and victory of conquest was on full display, which in turn symbolized the strength and continual expansion of the Roman Empire as well as the military prowess of the general.

The general himself was honoured as the embodiment of Jupiter, the chief Roman deity. The chariot would be drawn up to the temple of the Capitoline Jupiter where two white oxen would be sacrificed to the god. The purpose of the ceremony was to strengthen Rome's relationship to the gods, rather than the general's personal career. A slave would hold the laurel crown above his head and whisper continuously to the triumphant general, *momento mori,* remember you are mortal, to restrain any hubris in the *vir triumphalis.* However, we see ample examples of the Roman triumph being exploited for socio-political gain, notably under Augustus.

Source: *Alamy*

In Augustus' reign, few qualified for the triumph and he made sure that the triumph was only available for the imperial family and heirs. He limited the opportunity for generals to qualify and bolstered his own prestige. As such, the Roman triumph provides a historic lesson in regard to any society or institution's susceptibility to elite preservation. The generals usually fought in the imperial provinces, which were provinces that contained most of the Roman legions and which required constant attention owing to their highly turbulent political climate. In these provinces, there was greater potential for victories. The important senators would aim for these. Yet the qualification for a triumph was to have troops directly under one's command and, given that these were imperial provinces, the general would be commanding troops under the auspices of Augustus, and not his own. Augustus' rearrangement of the provincial command thereby deprived the senatorial class of any opportunity for a triumph, which exemplifies how the Roman triumph lost its military prestige to dynastic rule.

While an effective tenure followed by succession is the ultimate triumph, the board as decision maker leaves one's legacy at risk, complicating how one feels about the exit. During a tenure the CEO will, or should, collaborate with the board at the board's discretion. If a board is avoiding the succession the CEO may feel he or she has to prompt them. It would not be good practice for the exiting CEO to be directing the process, although in a family firm the individual may also be an owner, so have a more direct say. The most responsible approach for a departing CEO is to help prepare the way for the successor. The elements of the Succession Strategy Wheel, defined in this chapter, set out the tasks. They are primarily for the board, with the outgoing and new CEO involved as partners. Processes of loss and mourning, and internal rivalry for the top role, can be handled by an exiting CEO, who can legitimize conversational themes that might otherwise be seen as taboo, due to fear of conflict.

3.2 Board Strategy Practices

The strategy approach applied in this book builds on the emphasis of management author and adviser Henry Mintzberg and Joseph Lampel (1999) upon exploring the actual strategies — the actual doings — of top leaders. Further, rather than lofty ideas or slogan-type phrases, the practices should be described in a way that is crisp, clear and doable. It also makes it possible to identify these strategic processes across different strategic fields such as the governance field, leadership theory more generally, Human Resources (HR) and organizational development. Succession as a phenomenon falls within a convergence of these fields. None of them give a full picture but all are necessary and relevant.

A strategic practice approach to succession departs from what has been an excessive focus on how succession can go wrong. A strategy practice perspective is important for several reasons. It allows one to take some strategies beyond rules of thumb that might be misleading or just occasionally good suggestions. It makes it possible to see how the destructive and constructive succession dynamics are two sides of the same coin and to connect the dots with how failure in one succession strategy has implications for the execution of others. Importantly they do not give specific advice but are distinct strategy tasks that have to be addressed and where the outcome of each will be unique to the particular organization, time, context and challenges ahead. There are seven necessary strategies and this chapter identifies how each of them will counteract destructive group and individual dynamics.

From a group psychology process this is a bit surprising. An example is scapegoating that is an often-quoted destructive dynamic in succession. Groups scapegoat can be a very strong, and destructive, dynamic in ousting a leader or rejecting a leader on entry. It can also be a process that a top leader or a board uses to protect their own position. Scapegoating in groups is connected to maintaining the established cohesion of groups and evading accountability with either avoiding or triggering a succession. The added value of seeing this in a strategy practice perspective is what such processes, when they have happened or are in process, do to the strategic capacity of decision makers. Scapegoating will erode the capacity to review the past as one then would have to address this often taboo process. The implication is that a board or group of decision makers then with more difficulty can actually review achievements and strengths, what the organization is capable of and what it needs leadership to do. The link between the past and future is therefore fragmented and broken and one is less able to formulate a realistic expectation for the next leader. With scapegoating one also is in danger of doing the opposite, that is over-idealization, of a type of leadership or a specific leader.

Many consultant and isolated research advice suggest common sense steps and guidelines that play into elite preservation or unfounded guidelines. An example of the latter is the often suggested "best practice" that an outsider should be recruited if there is radical change necessary. The picture is more complex than that. Is someone who has been in the organization for three years an outsider or insider? Is someone who worked for many years in the business then left for another top leadership role an outsider or insider? What about personal leadership skills of an insider that knows where the resistance is and can motivate colleagues in a radical change? In that situation one does not have the financial, and more general motivational, cost of possibly having to dismiss an otherwise competent leadership team so as to implement radical change. Often this can reflect more of a symbolic act so as to create trust in the stock market than actually increasing the capacity of the organization to adapt. In addition, with increased diversity in the top of an organization it might be that there is more creative tension and with this more agility without having to rely on a strong external leader to break a stagnated or groupthink dynamic within the organization.

While the strategy knowledge of each of these is helpful it is, with succession, necessary to explore the actual practices of decision makers. I apply a difference between a practice and strategy formulation. There are seven succession practices of strategic nature that one has to do, or strategize. In itself there are no specific strategies suggested that would be recommended. The strategy practices in successions are challenges, or tasks, that need to be addressed and solutions created for. An example is the strategy practice of a succession pool. Should one have only internal candidates or external candidates for the top leadership role? Deciding on this question is the strategy practice of a succession pool, the deliberation of how to do it is the strategy formulation. The latter would address: Do we have a preference when candidates are equally good? How would the choice of an external candidate, matching but not better than our own, affect the motivation of our talent pool? How radical is the mandate? Would an external candidate be able to understand the cultural change; and would an internal candidate be able to do it? If the former tenure was a radical change one, would an internal candidate be better at continuity? These questions will not have obvious answers and will be the subject of discussion. They can be revised during a succession process. One can, during the process, be surprised by an unusually strong internal candidate or a weak external field of candidates, events can change one's thinking, etc. The outcome can be typical for the type of organization, or unique to a culture or organizational phase. The outcome may be culture-defining and of strategic importance.

It is important to notice that if one does not strategize, or deliberate on strategy practices, one will unavoidably do it in a passive way. For example, doing a deal with a new CEO is a part of the succession planning; without it a succession will not happen and if it is not a part of the discussion one might have the successor dictate the terms or one is resetting the past or a practice in one's sector. In and of itself that is not wrong but it should be a deliberate and active process. Without conscious strategy formulation, the risk is a process that is random or a reset of the past, which may not be appropriate. For organizations in a turbulent context this amounts to carelessness. A strategic intent for each of the strategy practices is essential.

3.3 The Succession Strategy Wheel

The seven strategies are either explicitly studied or implicitly assumed in a rich research tradition. The Succession Strategy Wheel responds to a consistent and general conclusion within the field:

> different [succession] studies appeared to be directed toward "different parts of the elephant", each dealing with a potentially important but relatively small part of the problem.
>
> (Le Breton-Miller et al., 2004, p. 305)

This quote vividly describes the limitations of the research on succession, and more generally in the leadership and governance field (Donaldson, 2012). A research dilemma is captured: if the study is broad, it is difficult to discern clearly defined variables that are precise enough for quantitative research; if it is narrow, other important variables will be missed and it has little to say about practical implications. Quantitative research will therefore, unavoidably, lead to important aspects being ignored and a lack of overview of the complexity of the processes. Qualitative research, with in-depth case studies over long time periods, allows for other types of theory development. It also allows for more practice-relevant theories.

A succession is brought forward by the following strategy practices. The succession practices are as follows:

1. Determining structure and succession system
2. Mandate of the next tenure
3. Wish list of leadership skills
4. Successor pool
5. Executive discretion
6. Making a deal
7. Handover.

Depending on internal and external factors, type of organization and former leadership tenures, the strategy formulations and outcome of each will be specific to the organization and its specific situation.

The Succession Strategy Wheel captures a complex process and, from a board perspective, is an *orchestrated process* that requires *steering* rather than a strict stage-based approach. A planned or sudden exit of a CEO means the board needs to make sure that the right structure and some succession system is in place. There will be differences across regulation, and cultures, that will have significance for the succession system. An exiting CEO in the USA is possibly also the chair of the board, and if this is the case an independent subcommittee will most probably determine the succession outcome. In a family business it might be an ownership forum that oversees the process. Lack of clarity over the authorizing structure will cause conflict and tension. A CEO exit might also be done together with other types of transitions, such as listing a business on the stock market, in which case the succession system and governance structure will change. The following strategy practices (see Figure 3.1), addressing different important tasks, are necessary for creating a succession outcome.

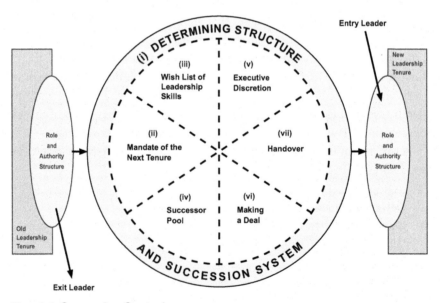

Figure 3.1 Succession Strategies

1. *Determining structure and succession system*: determining who the decision makers are is essential and might be taken for granted. Within most corporate governance structures in Europe, the board represents the decision makers. The actual task might be delegated to a subcommittee, and the chair of the board, or another board member, might be the leader of this subcommittee. I define the succession system as the structure and procedure for the process; this is discussed further in Chapter 6. Its legitimacy derives from how it secures a logic on leadership that is seen as trustworthy. In a non-family company this is often seen as a merit-based logic but, as I will show, the logic differs according to type of institutions. Even a logic of merit is not always straightforward.

2. *Mandate of the next tenure*: strategizing a mandate properly involves linking the past and future. In order for this to be achieved, it is necessary to analyse past mistakes and achievements so as to identify a gap. Former leaders might have had a huge impact on the culture and competence in the organization that one wants to maintain or radically change. Intrinsically, members of the board, employees and observers often have this as a starting point; what needs to be continued and what needs to be changed or developed from scratch.

3. *Wish list of leadership skills*: based on the latest in leadership theory, and the experience of seasoned leaders, the notion that certain leadership skills are universally good for any organization is fading. In his classic book *Searching for a Corporate Savior: The Irrational Quest for Charismatic CEOs* Rakesh Khurana (2004) portrays organizations as seeking an over-idealized image of leaders as heroic beings. With an over-reliance on glamorization and over-idealization wishful thinking has become a part of the succession dynamic. To marginalize leadership is wishful thinking a group can be caught up in. To counteract either an over-idealization or marginalization the mandate should be used as context for the leadership skills and qualifications one is seeking.

4. *Successor pool*: an important part of a succession process is identifying the candidates available. It helps to have continuous preparation to develop a pool of internal candidates, typically overseen by the HR department. As such it can be an ongoing process of leadership development within the business. A board might choose to align this with the new strategy when an actual succession is forthcoming. The available pool of

candidates, in most organizations, will influence the succession process (Allgood, 2003). The succession pool should be an ongoing concern for the board and is discussed more broadly in Chapter 7. It addresses the resource dependency, and competition, most organizations have in attracting talented potential top leaders.

5. *Executive discretion*: this defines the freedom of action the top leader has without seeking approval from the governing structure (Crossland & Hambrick, 2007). It may be changed in line with the mandate, or adjusted to the level of competence and demands of the successor. In Chapter 10 it is discussed more explicitly. Disagreements about executive authority can arise within leadership tenures and trigger a succession and can be due to excessive CEO discretion, hubris or narcissism (de Vries, 2019). See also Chapter 5. Another possible trigger for a CEO exit is that the board is micromanaging, or creating a strong mandate but not giving the executive discretion necessary for implementing the required changes.

6. *Making a deal*: matching organizational need and leadership drive, in the process of making a deal with the leader, is often taken for granted, but is an important succession practice. It is common sense that without a deal there is no succession process. At the same time the level of attention paid to this part of the process varies hugely between different types of organizations. It will also reflect to what extent the organization has a high degree of dependency, or few or only one candidate. Too high a degree of dependency on one candidate or a limited pool would undermine how strong the board or family is in the negotiations. Such resource dependency is a threat to the overall process. It leaves the organization prone to having to adapt to a leader's narcissistic needs at the onset of the tenure.

7. *Handover*: immersion or ejection of a leader. The handover is the actual exit–entry of the individual leaders. An exit and entry have an event to plan for and aftermath that often is discussed as the succession but here is seen as just a part of the process. The concept of a favourable transaction atmosphere has been discussed within the field. Family business research has referred to knowledge transfer in succession (e.g. Royer et al., 2008).

The *orchestrating* of the process is important. The strategy processes are therefore presented graphicly as a wheel, rather than a set of stages. An initial strategy practice is to review the past and future so as to synthesize an initial mandate and future course for the organization – to ask: What are the long-term scenarios and more fundamental questions about strategy? It might seem obvious, but it is important to have this discussion before starting to discuss the type of leader required. Avoiding a discussion leading to an agreed mandate will often open up tensions or disagreements about future challenges. If such possible conflicts are not addressed one can later discover one has three candidates representing different perspectives rather than the three best that all could be good candidates for an agreed mandate. The succession pool has thereby not been strategized so as to include candidates that could work toward a mandate or expectation. Such surprises and the need for correction in the process are often the case and a linear process is often not possible. Orchestrating means addressing the different strategies in an order that fits the situation but aligning, and revisiting, each of them as the process moves forward to a handover. They might move forward in discrete stages as each strategy formulation will possibly influence each other. Surprising candidates, or a limited set of available candidates, might cause an adjustment to the mandate. A radical mandate requires strong executive discretion (see Chapter 10).

Another aspect is the *steering* of the process. If it emerges, in the course of the execution of the different practice, that there is too much distrust or conflict, it may be necessary to redesign the actual process of planning the succession. The steering process is achieved by focusing on the strategy of each as they also counteract specific types of destructive group dynamics and individual ambitions and emotions. These need to be acknowledged, while maintaining a strong focus on the task at hand, and on maintaining organizational competitiveness. The board may be steering the process through what can be choppy, sometimes stormy, waters. Such dynamics are further described in detail in Chapters 4 and 5. The model can be used in a review or planning process, as it indicates the constructive efforts necessary and can identify the main threats that may erode the strategy formulation and chances of a good outcome.

3.4 Lame Duck Periods

Before a handover the exiting leader will often experience a period where his power and authority is diminished. The organization can drift and lose focus if this period is too long. A lame duck period can come at a critical time for the company, possibly related to the same issues that triggered the succession. A handover period should not be too long, though some time might be necessary, as there are both emotional and practical issues to consider. In the case of long notice periods, a lame duck period has to be seen in the context of whether there is turbulence in the market and the complexity of the role. The quality of the relationship between the new and exiting leader is important. If this is strong, and the candidate is internal, the lame duck period may be negligible. A troubled exit and mourning process, or rivalry, may create considerable problems. An exiting leader and the board have to take into account the discretional authority of the leader in the transition. The exiting CEO should consult with the entering CEO before the handover. The exiting CEO may take some of the less critical decisions; but they may still be consequential and would influence the next tenure. In exceptional circumstances the board may take the decision to avoid a leadership vacuum. Extended or poorly handled lame duck periods can create internal politics, which can become destructive as decisions get pushed forward or postponed. To mitigate the uncertainty, the board may decide to step in and make decisions in concert with the CEO in the lead-up to the handover. In some cases, the incoming CEO can face a significant build-up of decisions to take.

Boards should also have contingency plans for the sudden departure of the senior leader, owing to illness or death, or reasons such as fraud or corruption that mean that a CEO has to leave with immediate effect. Indeed, being prepared for such an eventuality is enough reason for treating succession as an ongoing responsibility, rather than an occasional activity. It could be incorporated into scenario planning, as part of risk assessment strategizing. Directors will need to know what to do in the event of an unplanned exit; there will typically be a designated member of the leadership team to act as interim in an emergency. Other considerations are offering support for managers and other employees in the event of shock and having to cope with loss. This could be the case regardless of the reason for a sudden departure. In the cases of dismissal owing to fraud or similar cause, the feelings may almost be akin to grief.

Practice summary

Leadership in Succession Process

These seven succession practices need to be aligned and they are best understood as interlinked, not isolated processes. It a process of *orchestrating* due to the complexity and alignment of the different outcomes as the process evolves. It is also a *steering* process where the group dynamics and emotional reactions have to be, at the minimum, acknowledged, and possibly managed. Groups such as a board, a top leadership team, stakeholders and the wider organization may struggle to overcome such group dynamics, and if they do not, this can have severe implications for the succession outcome. These group dynamics are described in Chapter 4. Likewise, individual emotions can derail or obstruct the process and also have to be managed by a board or chair of the board, or the exiting or entering CEO.

Strategy Formulation in Successions

Successions can be planned, or reviewed for their thoroughness, by focusing on the seven key strategies. Each of them has a set of strategic implications that need to be considered. The organization's major external threats, former achievements, culture, dependency on an internal or external pool of candidates, regulation, executive discretion, deal-making, resourcefulness, the prestige or allure of the role, in addition to handover themes, are all important. Chapter 6 elaborates on issues regarding determining structure and the succession system. Chapter 9 explores this theme within a family business context. The mandate, wish list of leadership skills and succession pool are described more in detail in Chapter 7, and handover in Chapter 8. Issues of executive discretion are discussed in Chapter 10, while the overall process and integration of these strategies are discussed as a trust issue for the board in Chapter 11.

References

Allgood, S., & Farrell, K. A. (2003). The match between CEO and firm. *The Journal of Business, 76*(2), 317–341.

Beard, M. (2009). *The Roman triumph*. Harvard University Press.

Crossland, C., & Hambrick, D. C. (2007). How national systems differ in their constraints on corporate executives: A study of CEO effects in three countries. *Strategic Management Journal, 28*(8), 767–789.

Donaldson, T. (2012). The epistemic fault line in corporate governance. *Academy of Management Review, 37*(2), 256–271.

Khurana, R. (2004). *Searching for a corporate savior: The irrational quest for charismatic CEOs*. Princeton University Press.

Le Breton-Miller, I., Miller, D., & Steier, L. P. (2004). Toward an integrative model of effective FOB succession. *Entrepreneurship Theory and Practice*, *28*(4), 305–328.

Mintzberg, H., & Lampel, J. (1999). Reflecting on the strategy process. *Sloan Management Review*, *40*, 21–30.

Royer, S., Simons, R., Boyd, B., & Rafferty, A. (2008). Promoting family: A contingency model of family business succession. *Family Business Review*, *21*(1), 15–30.

de Vries, M. F. K. (2019). *Down the rabbit hole of leadership*. Palgrave Macmillan.

4

THE FORCE OF GROUP DYNAMICS

Group dynamics, and the emotions they are associated with, can be very destructive for succession processes. In this chapter I will describe some of these dynamics, with an emphasis on how one can recognize them, and show how they are destructive. In western societies, Europe and the USA in particular, we have a cultural bias to ignore group processes. We have a tradition of thinking about ourselves as independent actors in the world, but this bias means that we may be unaware of group narratives or social pressures that are equally important. We have a strong belief that our minds are the creators of the decisions we make. Through our educational system we have often been trained to think we take autonomous decisions.

Organizations and their social structures, with their departments and hierarchies, are not empty structures but consist of a collection of individuals who constitute a group. In the context of a succession, the organization is best seen as several subgroups with different agendas, interests and identities. Some of their interests and agendas might be seen as being in conflict. The way in which the groups are structured, and subdivided, will evolve as the governance of the organization evolves. Should there be a difficult or failed succession the whole organization will be at risk, so an effective succession process is in the interests of the whole group. In the following I will describe succession as a constructive and necessary group dynamic that ensures the longevity of group membership. Several destructive group dynamics that are threats to the succession process ensuring such continuity are groupthink, scapegoating, elite preservation and over-idealization or marginalization of leaders or types of leadership. Throughout, and in the last section, I describe how one can recognize when one has been drawn into a group dynamic and lost some of one's individuality, self-reflection and critical thinking

4.1 Succession as Constructive Group Dynamic

It should be borne in mind when exploring destructive group dynamics that succession itself is a group dynamic, but one in which much media and other attention is focused on the individual. Succession is a process of safeguarding the future leadership and continuity of the group. Development of a governance function ensures this and is a constructive group dynamic. Governance is often seen as a legal or regulatory, hence very technical, field while here it is seen as the result of how a group and stakeholders create a structure that safeguards trust in the leadership of the organization. The details and intent behind procedures, such as a succession system, are important as they reflect group norms safeguarding trust. As I will show, the governing function can vary widely and work excellently for different groups and purposes. In all governing structures around a specific group of people with a task there will be a succession system as part of it.

The most vivid and relevant description of how such structures develop is often, in our age, shown when a venture starts to grow and needs some formality. The example of a growing and successful new venture provides an interesting window into succession dynamics at a more general level (see Ottolenghi case, Chapter 2). It shows how the founder group evolved into an organization. Inevitably a start-up firm has a high level of informality, with little differentiation of roles, formal structure for how they take decisions or formal systems creating accountability. At some point a venture will, to survive, become more efficient, roles need to be made clearer so as to reduce interpersonal conflicts and accountability needs to be created. There can be resistance from founders to greater formality as they fear losing the highly adaptable and innovative ways of working that have led to some success and growth. While some formalization will be necessary, resistance to overly formalized processes may be well founded, so the balancing act is delicate. Most organizations go through a maturing process, or similar significant change, as well as a succession process, which it may be linked to. As an example: when a company is listed on the stock-market, or delisted, nationalized or privatized, the change is such that the logic of leadership has to change. In most cases it will lead to the exit of a top leader or to a review of what type of leadership is needed. A shift from one type of governance to another involves redefining the type of succession capability that fits the new type of ownership and the new stakeholders. In this way our organizations are evolving from their founding and will change according to the historical context and social changes. I will later describe how such changes can lead to a shift in the leadership logic of the organization. Such disruptive succession triggers particularly strong group dynamics.

Ancient Greece and Rome, the cradle of European civilization, and their political and philosophical influence makes classicists such as Mary Beard relevant in how they can show it still influences our laws, types of institution and the tension between individuals and groups when institutions evolve (Beard, 2016). With regards to succession exits the most celebrated, or referred to, of all time is that of Julius Caesar. Fascination with this tale is no accident, for it illustrates perennial themes. It is the story of a public assassination, by an elite group of patrician senators – a group revolt against Caesar's attempt to build legitimacy around personal leadership at the expense of a group, and system, that was committed to having a strong sense of checks and balances. The senate system itself was crumbling, in a process that brought Caesar, a brilliant and ambitious general, to power (see Box 4.1, pages 50–51).

4.2 Groupthink

Groupthink became mainstream as a phenomenon in the wake of reviews into the causes of the financial crisis of 2008/09. The top leaders, often talked about as "Masters of the Universe", were carefully selected and highly paid – some would say, obscenely so – yet they failed completely. Much of the detail is highly technical, especially surrounding the creation of synthetic debt instruments where the ultimate assets against which they were valued were opaque or illusory. Cheap money and easy credit fuelled much speculation with unrealistic valuations (Whiteley, 2009). Ultimately,

BOX 4.1 FALL OF CAESAR

By Agnes Wilhelmsen

BRUTUS:
What means this shouting? I do fear the people
choose Caesar for their king.
CASSIUS:
Ay, do you fear it?
Then must I think you would not have it so.
BRUTUS:
I would not, Cassius, yet I love him well.

(Shakespeare, *Julius Caesar*)

This is one of Shakespeare's many plays that revolve around successions. This scene is just before Julius Caesar is assassinated in the senate house. The assassination of Julius Caesar was a culmination of conflict between the Optimates and the Populares, essentially a conflict between republican rule and military/dictatorial rule. This all began during the first triumvirate in 60 BCE. The political trio consisting of Julius Caesar, Crassus and Pompey emerged not out of fidelity but out of practicality, for each saw the advantages that the others could provide. This rather impromptu arrangement dominated politics in Rome and the alliance was further consolidated by Pompey's marriage to Caesar's daughter Julia in 59 BCE. Julia's death in 54 left Caesar and Pompey's relationship fragile. After Crassus' death in 53 the triumvirate was not only over, but Pompey and Caesar, re-absorbed as leaders of the rival political factions of Optimates and Populares, entered into greater civil strife.

Caesar, returning from Gaul, was ordered to disband his army (as was the custom of a general) yet he crossed the Rubicon with the army and so initiated the civil war. This ended in Caesar's victory at the battle of Pharsalia in 48. Brutus (a leading figure in Caesar's assassination) had been close to Caesar. He belonged to the plebeian *gens Junia*, one of the most acclaimed families of Rome. According to Roman legend the family's ancestor, Lucius Junius Brutus, had helped overthrow the last king of Rome Tarquinius Superbus who was also his uncle in 509 BCE. This marked the end of monarchy and introduced the Roman Republic.

Although Brutus had previously been close to Caesar, Caesar's growing conflict with the senate caused Brutus to side with Pompey at the battle of Pharsalia. Brutus appealed to Caesar for mercy and was granted amnesty by Caesar following the defeat against Pompey. However, Caesar's increasingly monarchical behaviour, notably in his role as dictator 'in perpetuity', led to a group of senators led by Brutus and Cassius assassinating the dictator in 44BCE.

Source: *Alamy*

the causes were behavioural and only a few actors understood what was going on. The ones who did would opportunistically use the groupthink of the others for their own profit. A summary of financial crises for *International Finance Review* concluded that their common features had been: "excessive exuberance, poor regulatory oversight, dodgy accounting, herd mentalities and, in many cases, a sense of infallibility" (Rhodes, 2011). The US Congress' Financial Inquiry Commission, reporting in 2011, concluded that the financial crisis was entirely avoidable (2011). Across several such investigations groupthink was seen as a principal cause for how these leaders would ignore, some knowingly, the risks they took.

From a succession point of view, deciding on a candidate from a cohesive in-group implies a belief of superiority and invulnerability of the group. This is often accompanied by closed-mindedness in collective rationalization, stereotyping of others than the elite, self-censorship and illusion of agreement. Defective decision making, due to groupthink, will be marked by an incomplete survey of alternatives and objectives, ignoring of risk, failure to revisit alternatives rejected, poor information research and selective bias in processing information (Rose, 2011). The different strategy practices described in Chapter 3 compensate for such flaws in decision making. In a board groupthink is, if it persists, destructive. A group uncritically loyal to a consensus can cause a lack of reality orientation and be trapped in a path dependency, or tunnel thinking, with regards to specific strategies.

Conversations by groups, when one investigates the experience of groupthink, has been described as "happy-talk" by thinkers Carl Sunstein and Reid Hastie (2014). They describe this as polite mannered, making sure everyone is comfortable and making sure no feathers are ruffled. It involves superficially harmonious conversations, but ones in which difficult problems are sidestepped and decisions made on superficial understanding. When dissenters stay mute, others mistake this silence for agreement. In hindsight it is described by members as: "Well, my thoughts were on another track when I had critical questions that I did not express or put out there." The double set of thoughts, saying something or nothing while thinking something else, is another signal of groupthink: "I thought that the strategy would not work but I did not say so as there was a majority in favour," or "Why am I not more excited about this course of action? I'm not sure the risks are understood, but all the others seem very confident, I don't know if it is necessary to challenge it." Self-censoring and double thinking in this way – happy talk – can create uncomfortable feelings; cynicism might follow if one does not have the courage to speak out.

When in a group, you may consider yourself as an autonomous individual, but the reaction of the group to your thoughts and actions will be ever-present. This will have an emotional element. In the cases where we disagree with the dominant view, there might be concerns around expressing dissent: fear of disapproval, hostility and rejection. When these fears are dominant in a significant number of members, groupthink can emerge. Informal and formal leaders will regulate this, tipping the group towards or away from tolerating dissent.

4.3 Scapegoating

In 1960 Gursky became one of the first researchers in social science to address succession (Rowe et al., 2005). He investigated succession processes in basketball teams and the replacement of the coach. He observed that when a team was performing badly and the coach was sacked, performances rarely improved after he was replaced. Gursky suggested that a ritual scapegoating of a leader would lead to worse performances for the organization. This research highlighted the importance and the risks of ritual scapegoating, but was later critiqued, rightly, for not being a general explanation, and for failing to account for successions that were successful. While not being a phenomenon capturing the succession dynamics in full, one can see incidences where a succession takes place, but it is not clear that a different leader would respond better to the strategic challenges or threats. An initial exit based on scapegoating can result in a "CEO revolving door", with top leaders exiting and entering after a short interval. Scapegoating is a seductive process and a consultant, or advisor, working with groups skilled in scapegoating can become an easy target oneself. At some point this process would lead to the chair of the board having to leave. Few chairs of boards can stay in the role with two or more failed CEO successions on their watch.

Scapegoating can be a quite obvious process to an observer but less so to the group. The origin of the term scapegoating informs us of why it is often driven by unconscious individual and group dynamics and why it can be experienced as temporarily pleasant. It comes from an old tribal tradition where the ritual was for a community to seek redemption from its sins. The ritual was to write down one's sins on a piece of paper, or some variation of this, and attach it to a goat. The goat was sent out into the wilderness to die. As cruel and superstitious ritual it illustrates the pleasure of avoiding blame and feeling guilt-free. Once the scapegoat has left, the others can start again, as new. When one is in the middle of a group that is scapegoating, one is preoccupied with the view that the group has been victim of the scapegoat's failures. It justifies the anger and can be an outlet for at least verbal aggression. For anyone who is scapegoated, such processes are painful and, in the worst cases, traumatizing. For the rest of the members of the group it comes as a relief, possibly with a bit of excitement and can push them forwards. Groupthink is different as, for most seasoned leaders, it is with some discomfort they censor themselves or revert to happy talk.

It is important to note that if a board scapegoats, or ignores and sanctions it within the organization, it will have a limited desire to analyse the past. Scapegoating erodes the capacity to synthesize, and revisit, mandates throughout the process. A board might focus, instead, on defining an overidealized image of a new leader that a headhunter is going to provide them with. Both scapegoating and overidealization of a leader or leadership reflect wishful thinking. It is as if there were a leader out there, someone infallible, who can save the organization. A mandate created by a scapegoating group will often be conceived as "anything but someone like the last CEO", with an overemphasis on past leaders' individual faults and weaknesses.

As discussed in Chapter 3 the formulation of an expectation, or a mandate, is necessary for the succession process. It also protects from future scapegoating as it ensures a focus on reviewing the past in a level-headed way, where more complex analysis of causes for a leadership failure can be explored. There are implications if the exit of a CEO has been driven by scapegoating and the board were unable to stop it. It is, of course, very possible that the leader's performance actually was substandard. The strategy formulation when finding a new leader, so as to avoid ritual scapegoating, should focus on an appropriate mandate, which acknowledges a wider range of factors that contributed to the mistakes of the past. In the same way, if a revered and loved CEO is exiting, there will also have been others who contributed to the success. And there are always lost opportunities and smaller mistakes to learn from. Such analysis is a good strategy practice in its own right, and also has the benefit of counteracting potential scapegoating of a new CEO.

4.4 Elite Preservation

A strand of research, based on sociological studies of leadership, has explored how an elite group behaves in leadership roles, and how it retains its power. Elites will develop, and are necessary, in any organization or community. This is also, at the organizational level, discussed as the upper echelon of the organization (Magee & Galinsky, 2008). The upper echelon within an organization can be isolated or have social bonds to a broader elite outside the organization. New and modern elites develop through education and universities, through membership groups, through neighborhoods and other social networks. Over time the process creates a network of members that will develop a sense of group and individual identity. While elites are necessary what is destructive in a succession context is if the group excludes individuals who are different, or fails to exclude insiders who don't perform according to the stated criteria. Elites have risen and fallen through history, and the institutions they governed and led have fallen with them.

Elites, or the upper echelon in an organization, can convince themselves that they need to act to preserve their status and prestige and this will, over time, create a sense of supremacy, or other rationales, justifying a sense of entitlement. They display collective emotions, have frequent interaction and observe rituals, maintaining social bonds. As such, the elite tends to act and think as one in response to events within the organization or the group. The researcher Magee reviewed how elites preserve themselves and found that internal cohesion, and identification with similarities, makes the elite cohesive (Magee & Galinsky, 2008). A narrative, often idealizing a certain type of leadership, knowledge and perspective, makes them tend to reproduce themselves. The price to pay, or long-term cost, is that elites become stagnant and less innovative. In particular, defining who is entitled to become candidates in the pool of potential leaders is often an important dynamic for elites.

Upper echelons that aim to preseve are damaging or stifling for an organization and to some extent they are inevitable. What is unhealthy is the cohesion and self-preservation so that it is difficult for others to enter into the elite. To have social mobility in and out of elites prevents stagnation. Considerable effort is needed as not only will new ideas about entitlement be accepted but some members of an elite and the top of the organization will have to be set aside or excluded and the loss of entitlement triggers anger and possibly rage. A law in Norway, implemented in 2003, requiring all public boards to have 40% of their members be women, represents such an effort. It is the duty of a board to ensure discussion that is both broad and deep, to encourage dissent, to challenge dominant thinking. This is encouraged by ensuring diversity of background, both within the board and on the shortlist of individuals for executive posts. Here many headhunters have been slow to react. The following is a quote from Anne Carine Tanum, Chair of the Board of DNB in Norway for ten years. During her tenure the bank improved its position from being number three in the Scandinavian market to number one.

The selection committee for board members are in Norway often set down by the general assembly; not the board itself. They were diligent in recruiting women for board roles. A representation from each of the two biggest owners was at the board, then three others chosen from the wider business community. They also made sure that it was members from other backgrounds than finance. Overall we also had more variation in the age of board members. With the image banking had all this was important.

As board we wanted to increase the numbers of female leaders in all the leadership levels, including the top leadership. Our CEO at that time, a man by the way, was all in support of this and did a great job. The board insisted that he had, for members of his leadership team, a short list of four candidates where half were women. Inside the organization the CEO would have two final candidates one of them a woman for every leadership role, no exception. If it weren't the position would stay vacant.

Men tell me it will ruin the business − I show them our results and they have noting to argue with. Others argue − some women − they don't want to be chosen due to some quota but due to competence. What does that mean? You are selected from half the population! I don't have a problem with that. There are a lot of very competent women out there if you start looking. Of course people such as headhunters would say that they don't exist. This was in the beginning. It just meant it was more difficult. With the rate of women in higher education it was of course possible. Our CEO found many very talented leaders a bit further down in the organization and they are now excellent and hard-working leaders.

We have now had this policy for ten years and have one of the highest rates of female representation in the finance sector. We have over this period been top of the class profit-wise. But we were systematic and the selection committee, the board and the CEO were signaling the same thing. His successor, the new CEO, is a woman. It was a systematic effort as it also had to be 50% women in the trainee, leadership and educational programs. Now, when we select law firms to work with we put up as a condition that they have at least one female partner as part of the team. This is now extended to architect firms and other service providers.

Executive successions are used as one of the mechanisms keeping an elite in place. Often unwittingly a pool of candidates that emerges from consultation with headhunters has in the past gravitated towards homogeneity. Increasingly this prompts criticism of lack of diversity regarding race and gender. Academic research has confirmed that elite preservation, often in a tacit, unspoken way, limits the available pool of candidates for senior posts, reducing diversity and weakening meritocracy. From a succession practice point of view, it is important to have a strong debate about how boards, the top leadership systems in organizations and possibly headhunters are unwittingly excluding diversity in the pool of candidates. In family-owned companies, increased education and leadership experience of women are triggering major changes in successions. This will be discussed further in Chapter 9.

4.5 Idealization and Marginalization of Leadership

Dynamics discussed in this chapter contribute to reducing the strategic possibility of a succession transition and can reveal some illusions, or wishful thinking (Khurana, 2004), about leaders or leadership. It is important to acknowledge the key skills and experiences successful leaders need to have. Bearing that in mind, succession dynamics can become too focused on the individual leader or a particular leadership style, at the expense of other equally important aspects of the process. There are two polarities: idealization and awe of a type of leadership or marginalizing, seeing leadership as not important. An awe-inspired relationship with the top leader can have its origin in earlier experiences that result in an expectation of compliance and conformity to authority figures. Certain education backgrounds or clubs and limited access memberships can be narratives that keep an idealized leadership style linked to a particular elite.

The polar opposite is exhibited by employees or other leaders who have a contrarian attitude. While these types of relationship can occur, most of us, in order to be able to work efficiently and constructively within complex organizations, have found a place of relative autonomy in between these polarities, where we appreciate a leader without being uncritical. Marginalized leadership is something one can encounter in any organization such as successful and innovative entrepreneurs or within the university sector.

Again some research from the classics, as well as continuing fascination with the rise and fall of the Roman Empire, can illuminate this point. The emperor Marcus Aurelius sought a major change in the succession by nominating his son (see Box 4.2). Many of our vilified and idealized ideas and myths about leadership come from historical periods, as do our legal and political structures.

BOX 4.2 MERITOCRATIC SUCCESSION AND ROMAN EMPIRE DECLINE?

By Agnes Wilhelmsen

Marcus Aurelius' reign as Roman emperor was from 161 until 180 CE and he pronounced his son Commodus as his successor. This concluded the Nerva-Antonine dynasty (96–192 CE), after a series of seven emperors, the first five of whom were known as The Five Good Emperors (Nerva, Trajan, Hadrian, Antonius Pius and Lucius Verus). The prosperity of this period has by research been attributed to how the emperors, rather than having a son as successor, would instead adopt a talented relative or member of the army. Marcus Aurelius, himself a brilliant man and successful emperor, broke with this custom and it is seen as a major factor in the decline of the Roman Empire.

Marcus Aurelius maintained good relations with the senate and engaged effectively in administrating the public affairs of the empire. His reign was also marked by military conflict. In 160–170 CE there were Parthian invasions, which the Emperor resisted, along with the Antonine plague, which caused a steep decline in the population throughout the Roman Empire. Marcus Aurelius spent the last years of his life campaigning in what is modern-day Germany, during which time he wrote his *Meditations* (170–180 CE). Writing in Greek he reflects on his everyday experiences and relates it to service, death and equanimity. With an engagement with Stoic philosophy he became known as The Philosopher by contemporary biographers. As such he is a prominent example of the philosopher king, a term in Plato's *The Republic*. His reign was perceived in a very positive light, particularly in comparison to that of his son and successor, Commodus.

The accession of Commodus can be seen as a restoration of the conventional father/son succession, yet the re-establishment of dynastic, monarchical succession was short-lived. Commodus was assassinated in 192. During his reign from 177–192 CE (the first three years as co-emperor with his father) Commodus showed little interest in administrative affairs and left the state's governance to his favourites. Commodus' dictatorial approach to the role of emperor caused the elite and the senate to fear and loathe him. His apparent narcissism and extravagant public games and shows gained Commodus popularity among the military, praetorian guard and common people. His own fervent participation in gladiatorial games, self-aggrandizement as a divine descendant of Romulus and taxing of the senate to fund such entertainment, increased his unpopularity in the senatorial context, culminating in his assassination.

Another factor was the influence of the praetorian guard, just one of the many groups that would try to establish themselves as an elite, or in control, through influencing the succession of emperors. During Emperor Augustus' reign there was a praetorian guard, a select force of bodyguards from the Roman army. Their purpose was to protect the emperor. During the imperial period they intervened in politics, interrupting the adoptive system of succession through what was effectively a military coup d'état. The Emperor Caligula was resented by many but in particular by Cassius Chaerea a member of the praetorian guard whose high voice Caligua would ceaselessly mock. In 37 CE he was assassinated by the praetorian guard led by none other than Chaerea himself. Having removed an emperor, the Guard found themselves in need of a new one so as to preserve their position. They kidnapped Claudius, Caligula's uncle, who had been hiding in the imperial household. The Guard hailed Claudius as their emperor, probably quite pleased by how indebted to them this new emperor would be.

Source: *Alamy*

4.6 Acknowledgement and Participation

Group dynamics are elusive processes to understand when one is in the middle of them. For an observer, or outsider point of view, it can be more obvious and clear. Their force is due to how they draw one in and it is most likely an evolutional phenomena. To have group cohesion has been important but it also makes one lose one's sense of individuality and critically review one's own actions. Most people, experts and top leaders in particular, like to think about themselves as having a good grasp of themselves and as being a leader. Social psychology has shown that top decision makers, as everyone else, get caught up in group dynamics and that it is a subconscious process. By unconscious I mean that it is possible to understand one's part in it if one can identify it in precise terms, often through the involvement or talk with someone from the outside. The different group dynamics will make one feel different; groupthink creates a sense of unease as one cannot voice concerns or, if one is in the lead, a sense of efficiency and control. It is an overall destructive group dynamic that can be kept in place by the others described here. Scapegoating makes one feel strong and often creates, while one is in the middle of it, a good feeling. Elite preservation makes you feel safe and privileged and one can have the right to be offended by scrutiny. Idealization of leadership triggers admiration and a sense of gratefulness and is possibly one of the group dynamics that are most influenced by one's own need from early life.

Group dynamics can lose their power over individuals if they are openly acknowledged. There is often a taboo around group dynamics and hence they are not acknowledged. Only in hindsight does it seem they can be recognized unless one has a strong outsider or member forcing the issue. The taboo is kept in place by informal or formal leaders sanctioning anyone who raises it to the members' awareness. It can have various rationales such as saving face, framing it as trivial or not relevant while the members of the group use an added rationale that it is an over-complication, it is not time or is ridiculed or just ignored. These are warning signals and indicate that a taboo is in place – if one feels uncomfortable raising an issue it might be due to destructive group dynamics. Raising something that is irrelevant in a healthy and dynamic group does not bring with it the same feeling of being uncomfortable or a bit of a nuisance. One just said something not useful and it did not therefore implicate a sanction. Another good indicator is that one gets increasingly disturbed by not finding it easy to raise an issue and is starting to mention it, and find support, in informal contexts or outside the group.

Practice summary

Diagnosis of Group Dynamics

To identify and prevent groupthink is important. It is often fuelled by elite preservation, earlier scapegoating and either an idealization or marginal-ization of leadership. In particular, in succession, these dynamics should be acknowledged and attended to. During a succession, the board and chair of the board are more operative in decision making compared with other times, when their role is more one of monitoring, or dialogue with, the CEO.

Prevention

The leader of the board should be impartial and refrain from stating personal preferences. Each member should have the duty to be a critical evaluator of the group's work, and a climate of giving and accepting critical questions should be encouraged by everyone. One can set up a subgroup, such as a selection committee, that makes proposals and is in dialogue with the board. Several subgroup discussions can be used to challenge assumptions, raise issues and broaden the range of topics explored. It should be possible for members to discuss issues with outsiders, provided measures are taken to ensure confidentiality. If the process is too sensitive, outsiders should be brought in for a review or to reflect on the process. An important con-sideration is that a headhunter might easily be a part of an elite, and share a certain notion of idealized leadership in addition to having a business model based on dependency and an established network of leaders they are in contact with. Many female chairs in my research have been very explicit about the issue of unconscious bias (see chapter 6), which can be at play when there is not more diversity in the candidates in an initial pool, or among the last three candidates.

One member of the group can be the devil's advocate; challenging assumptions that are being tacitly made. Following a method and disciplined approach is useful, including checklists for the process. It is worth bearing in mind that if one has already failed in a succession process, or has some of the blame for a failed leadership tenure, the board and chair may be in denial of their contribution. In this situation the incoming leader can be under severe stress, and groupthink and scapegoating are even more likely to happen. Public scrutiny and time pressure add to this.

References

Beard, M. (2016). *SPQR*. Edizioni Mondadori.

The Financial Crisis Inquiry Report, US Government Commission report, January 2011. http://fcicstatic.law.stanford.edu/cdn_media/fcicreports/ fcic_final_report_full.pdf

Khurana, R. (2004). *Searching for a corporate savior: The irrational quest for charismatic CEOs*. Princeton University Press.

Magee, J. C., & Galinsky, A. D. (2008). Social hierarchy: The self-reinforcing nature of power and status. *The Academy of Management Annals*, 2(1), 351–398.

Rhodes, W. (2011). *Banker to the world: Leadership lessons from the front lines of global finance*. Tata McGraw-Hill Education.

Rose, J. D. (2011). Diverse perspectives on the groupthink theory–a literary review. *Emerging Leadership Journeys*, 4(1), 37–57.

Rowe, W. G., Cannella Jr, A. A., Rankin, D., & Gorman, D. (2005). Leader succession and organizational performance: Integrating the common-sense, ritual scapegoating, and vicious-circle succession theories. *The Leadership Quarterly*, 16(2), 197–219.

Shakespeare, W., *Julius Caesar*, 1.2.85–89. Available from http://shakespeare. mit.edu/julius_caesar/full.html

Sunstein, C. R., & Hastie, R. (2014). Making dumb groups smarter. *Harvard Business Review*, 92(12), 19.

Whiteley, P. (2009). *Strategic risk and reward: Integrating reward systems and business strategies after the credit crisis*. Thomson Reuters.

5

MANAGING FEELINGS AND EMOTIONS

A governing structure and succession process should create trust. Regardless of how it is designed it is also there to protect a group or business from destructive individual emotions. Governance theory and practice therefore has a focus on rationality, concentrating on procedure and legal aspects. I will in this chapter explore what emotions are particularly relevant for succession processes and what can be done to avoid them becoming the dominating feature and obstructing strategic thinking. Through the chapter I will describe loss and mourning, rivalry and hubris as processes driven by individual needs and interpersonal dynamics that can influence succession processes. Hope, in addition to trust, are the good emotions a careful process should aim for.

A healthy and partly unavoidable trio of emotions in CEO exits are sadness and loss, mourning and new hope. A good succession can trigger such emotions for the exiting leader or the organization. A sinister and destructive trio of emotions can also emerge: rivalry, narcissism and anger. They have been the subject of Shakespearian tragedy and are also present in modern organizations. What is already a difficult and sensitive process can, with small slights or an accumulation of emotional tension, suddenly flip, unleashing powerful emotions such as rage, envy, rivalry and greed, which then spiral out of control. In this chapter I will use the succession case of Pimco and the derailed exit process of Bill Gross. It illustrates the complexity of strong emotions on what seemed to be a planned and relatively constructive exit. Such cases, if they are research or client cases, are almost impossible to write about. I had just briefly been professionally helping someone within the organization but not in relation to this process. Due to a court filing from Gross, with detailed descriptions and transcripts from a meeting, one can get rich information about his view. Further lawyers' filings and the process within Pimco, also in the public domain, show a process that seemed to contain many of the typical destructive emotions that derail succession processes. I hope I have offered a balanced description that also was checked with an insider and employee. Everyone involved seems to have been overwhelmed by strong emotions and their own justification. They lacked insight into how they themselves contributed to a negative dynamic. Later in the chapter I will also describe the healthy emotions that a successions triggers.

5.1 Pimco: Failure in Care

The following case is, despite the destructive dynamics triggered by different leaders, a story that illustrates that the ultimate responsibility is on the governing body, here Allianz as the owner. The drama is triggered by strong emotions and avoidances, but ultimately it was down to the fact that Allianz stopped being effective in taking care of their own and Pimco's interests. As owner it allowed itself to be outmanoeuvred. It showed a lack of care in not executing its role to determine succession outcomes and enforce an agreement. It lost its role as owners and in that way was careless. Care is needed to enable a process and demonstrate thoughtfulness while also being strong on boundaries and dialogue. In many ways these are capabilities we often associate with female leadership. It is not something where one positions oneself as a strong leader or hero but where one must focus on achievements and the subtlety of managing a process where the exiting leader, the organization and a new leader are in focus. An essential part of care is often to be present but remain a bit anonymous and to make sure emotions don't spiral out of control.

Pimco was, and still is at the time of writing, an influential and major investment company in the bond market. Bill Gross founded the business in 1971 and was regarded within the financial sector as a peer of other legendary investment figures such as George Soros and Warren Buffet. He was sometimes dubbed the Bond King, and his reputation continued after the sale of Pimco to Allianz in 2000. His newsletter was read widely, including within governmental finance sectors as they would look for signs regarding their own bond issues. Pimco retained its influence through being the biggest investor for major private clients, insurance companies, sovereign funds and pensions funds.

In 1999 Gross had sold a majority stake in Pimco to Allianz and ceased to be the founder-owner. He transitioned to the role as Chief Investment Officer and would continue, within Pimco and the financial markets, as the highest authority on the bond market, with an influence that extended to government as well as investment decisions. Rather than taking out profit as an owner he received remuneration that was results based, including very generous bonuses, as was standard practice in the sector. So far so good. Eventually Allianz wanted to expand into other sectors such as equity investment, and it was at this point that disagreements emerged over strategy. Bill Gross disagreed with the diversification, wanting to continue as bond specialists. Such disagreements are common at the top of a business and need not have led to crisis, but there were warning signs of a more serious split. In one half-year period Gross' performance was below his usual level and concerns began to grow with key people inside Pimco. His deputy Mohamed El-Erian, a noted bond adviser with a high profile in his own right, quit the business in early 2014, citing problems with Gross' management style. Concerned over both management style and performance, the Allianz board began to negotiate with Gross on a plan and a package for his departure.

In 2013 and 2014 Pimco's board, with Allianz, prepared an exit with Bill Gross in what seemed to be a constructive path. An exit deal had been negotiated that made strategic and personal sense for Gross, Allianz and Pimco, but the succession process collapsed in a critical meeting. A representative from Allianz and Gross was to meet with three of the top leaders within Pimco to present the plan. One claim in the story was that the three "lieutenants" were afraid that having Gross around for even a short exit period might damage Pimco's reputation. Gross claimed that greed set in. The lieutenants refused to accept the plan and would not accept the deal, threatening to resign. This made Allianz's representative ineffective in enforcing the deal and in effect it became a coup against Gross and Allianz. It was also ensured that Gross would not be entitled to about $300 million in bonuses and, according to the bonus rules, it would be divided among the rest of the team. The consequences were grave. Gross quit Pimco in September 2014, and subsequently brought forward a $200 million lawsuit, accusing the cabal of Pimco lieutenants, with other partners, of seeking to divide his 20% share of the bonus pool between them. The latter had been given to Gross in the initial deal between Gross, the Pimco board and Allianz. Pimco resisted the lawsuit, citing poor performance by Gross and concerns over his management style. The two sides settled in March 2017 for $81 million.

The case illustrates how suddenly, without the steering hand of a board to contain emotions, the process flipped and spiralled out of control. The natural processes of loss, mourning and the creation of new hope were disrupted and rivalry, greed and strong individual ego needs took over, leading to a destructive transition.

5.2 Accepting Grief and Mourning

For a founder like Bill Gross, or anyone who enjoys a role for a relatively long time, there is more than likely going to be a sense of loss in exiting such a role. As is often advised it is a transition for the individual that needs to be well prepared. Sadness and mourning are necessary for moving on and such feelings must be borne. After some time, energy and hope for new types of roles and activities will return. One might think one is strong and will not have to address it but loss is an unavoidable neurobiological process (Panksepp & Biven, 2012). Board members and employees, and other leaders, might need to mourn a leader within the organization. An initial reaction of protest followed by a sense of loss can be felt not only over a departed individual or role; it can be protest and loss of a relationship, an icon or image, or an identification, any of which may have created a sense of safety. The pioneering psychologist John Bowlby (1980), who studied the importance of emotional and relational attachments for both children and adults, developed a concept of attachment as being very much in a group perspective. Without this primary affect and emotion we would not survive as a species because it makes sure we hold onto relationships and seek safety from danger. Loss and mourning therefore are also highly relevant in change processes and when one's identity is changing. This shows how roles are an important aspect of how we create identities.

The succession of a top leader, if it is an unplanned one, can trigger a short burst of denial, even panic, for employees, senior leaders and board members. If one is to leave a role with just a few days' or weeks' notice, more time will most likely be necessary to handle what can be felt like a shock, and sense of confusion, before the new reality is accepted and can be mourned. Some CEO roles are in volatile markets or the organizations are in a politically turbulent context. The top leader might be well advised to be prepared for a sudden dismissal. If a sudden exit is followed by passivity or a lack of strategic processes, the departure can be followed by despair. For less significant losses, recovery can be within two or three days. The exit of a top leader can also trigger a longer period of loss and mourning. In this regard the way an exit is handled is significant. For the exiting leader the transition can be to a new and attractive role and less mourning is necessary. Eventually, through discussion and renewal of strategy, one can create new visions and hope for one's future. Such new hope is therefore also the background for general advice to top leaders exiting from an active and rewarding career and top leadership role; plan your retirement well in advance and create specific plans and projects.

The board and the leader should acknowledge that the exit is associated with an individual loss of a role. In the terms of reference of attachment theory, there is also a loss of such ones bond to and identity invested in social and physical environment of the work, social identity, knowledge and skills one uses that give a sense of achievement. When the loss of a role becomes a public event, discussed in the business news or in local communities, the impact is commensurately significant to all involved. One's family can be drawn in and it can be a test for personal relationships. A sense of being unfairly treated, humiliated and shamed may have to be dealt with; it will affect the reputation of the organization as well as of the leader. Loss and sadness can in themselves often trigger denial and anger. When there is a mixture of emotions the impact can be even more profound. The practices often referred to — of dignified exits, acceptable retirement plans, space for mourning — are more than social niceties, they are significant for enabling effective succession.

Within a family business there is the additional impact for the exiting leader who has a dual role in the business and family; and on other family members as they adjust to their new roles and the new reality. Sometimes the mourning is very real; in a family firm, succession may be caused by the death of a dear family member and leader. Acknowledgment of loss and the necessity of some mourning are natural and healthy human processes. Loss and mourning processes are not destructive processes in themselves, as long as they are acknowledged and space is created to deal with them. Only a denial, or lack of awareness, can derail or obstruct a succession process. Important in being able to care and protect strategy processes is empathy with the need for loss and mourning. Developing such a capability represents a precious asset for top executives and the board.

5.3 Hope

The concept of change always being resisted is a simplified notion, because change can generate curiosity and the promise of renewal. In so far as it holds some validity, research indicates that the strongest resistance relates to mourning that which is lost, rather than resisting that which is new (Grady et al., 2019). When appropriate mourning has taken place, and one is not sad any more, the mind will start other emotional processes that are necessary for being motivated and energetic about the future. Different employees and other leaders will need different amounts of time. Some might not mourn a leader's exit, or even their own, and may have to hold back a sense of excitement at the new possibilities opened up by a CEO's exit. The board and top leaders' creation of a vision for the future can trigger some excitement and new drive; moreover it can be a fresh impetus that is positive – not just restoring a state of feeling safe. It can involve the excitement of curiosity, the fun in developing new strategies with others, often in a playful way. Just as loss and mourning and the experience of sadness are biologically hard wired in the brain, so are excitement, curiosity and the fun in playfulness with new ideas and possibilities (Solms, 2015). Care for such processes is to enable and bring a group or individual forward while taking a step back. More broadly about cares, in addition to enabling hope a board needs to care for the emotions the process triggers, so as to ensure efficient strategy processes. See Chapter 11 on further discussion on the care role to a board.

In and of itself a mourning process relieves the mind by revisiting, in the worst cases obsessing about, the past, but also enabling new paths to be visualized, building on new hope or visions. New paths might be rejected if sadness still prevails. Yet there can be a sense of excitement, of being curious about possibilities and in exploration of new ventures by a new leader, especially if supported by the board. An exiting CEO will have to accept this process and, in the later part of the his or her tenure, prepare the ground.

5.4 Rivalry at the Top

Veterans of the Bill Gross era report his highly eccentric and unpredictable manner, and this must have triggered anger and resentment in a group with highly competitive members. In itself it was a leadership strategy as unpredictability triggers a sense of high alertness, tension and a need to compensate for whatever vulnerabilities and insecurities members of the team might have. He would sit among the traders with his desk in an open plan office. On one occasion, he had received a box of doughnuts, stood up to distribute some of them to various desks, in silence and with great cere- mony, placing one on some colleagues' desks but not others', apparently at random, with uncertainty as to whether one was favoured by receiving this unexpected gift, or singled out for some other reason. Then, still without saying anything, he sat down again. He insisted on quietness in the office. At corporate parties, he would be the charming host, greeting everyone personally. In such a way he would be both close to and at a distance from his team members.

Competition and rivalry have often, within common language and within business studies, been seen as the same type of process. The threat of rivalry, also hyper-competition, is widely recognized in family businesses. Sibling relationships, but also different generations, can display rivalry that can deteriorate and lead to toxic succession processes (Osnes, 2016). In this section, I shall make a distinction between friendly competition, which is inevitable and healthy when individuals are vying for a role, and unhealthy rivalry, where personal animosity is on display. Rivalry is a very unpleasant feeling and is it also very concrete. Rather than competing about being seen as better – often by trying to win a prize – rivalry is more obses- sive and it can be pursued as if no creative options are possible. The diffe- rence between competition and rivalry is arguably a question of degree. Competition becomes personal rivalry when an individual is going much further than legitimately seeking a position, and is motivated by a sense of personal anger, revenge or "deathly" animosity. Intensely personal rivalry can waste time and resources, create a toxic work environment, polarize and damage working relationships and may promote unethical behaviour. Narcissism will be discussed in the next section; it is relevant here to make the point that it can have the same origin as rivalry: a sense that something is lacking and, most often at the unconscious level, that what one creates by oneself is not enough or good enough.

From a perspective of understanding the succession process, and how a board and an organization's leaders interact, awareness of the risk of rivalry is important. Rivalry can emerge between the chair and CEO, and can trigger a power-struggle and CEO exit. The chair may be in a position of being able to dismiss the CEO, but he or she would need the backing of the board. The chair's relationship with a CEO is fundamental for the board, as well as the CEO, in order to be effective. Different non-executives or executive board members may have preferred candidates for a top leadership post that can trigger rivalry within an internal pool of candidates or with the top leader. More obvious is the potential rivalry between individuals in the internal leadership pipeline, positioning themselves as candidates for the most senior executive role. An incoming leader may also have a rivalry with the departing leader. I will in Chapter 7 discuss how a legacy left behind by an incumbent can be felt as overwhelming and be a target of rivalry for new top leaders.

5.5 Vulnerability behind Narcissism

Even for only moderately narcissistic leaders, when an exit is involuntary, it will be felt as an insult. Emotional pushback might occur in addition to, or instead of, the normal processing of loss and mourning. For some, support and help can be important, but can be seen as a dependency that often is experienced as a humiliation if one is overly narcissistic. From a board's perspective it is important to remember that a top leader's degree of narcissism is not static; it may increase as a person comes into a position of power. A strong board, with clear guidelines and strong members and chair, can contain the individual and manage a moderately narcissistic leader. Throughout our civilization, shown through some of the contributions from the classical world in this book, narcissism and hubris constitute perhaps the main threat that governing structures need to curb.

Ideally, in the selection of a leader, those who are overly narcissistic, despite how seductive and charming they can be, should be avoided. The judgment is difficult, as some highly effective leaders can also be rather narcissistic. It is most accurate to conceive of narcissistic traits as a continuum and not as an either/or. Positive self-regard and confidence are perfectly healthy and necessary for a senior position. One can have a healthy self-image as well as a need for encouragement and confirmation. The more destructive narcissistic top leaders are more obsessive about praise, do not accept critique or disagreement, find faults in others and see and present themselves in only a positive, even heroic, light. Employees and leaders around a narcissistic leader might succumb to idealizing the leader or feel marginalized where their effort and achievements are ignored. They are often justified to have such an experience and it might lead to idealization of the top leader, to cynicism and for other employees and leaders to leave the organization. If the pathology becomes severe, and such a leader pursues hubristic strategies, the board might not have a choice, and would have to end their tenure. It might be a sad process for the board as the leader may have been very efficient and innovative in the beginning of the tenure. Within the organization a very narcissistic leader can start projects that are unrealistic, erode work ethic, culture and values and lead to a brain drain of talented people.

There are other difficult behaviors that CEOs who are narcissists exhibit: they nurture rivalries and can act out of rage if they feel they have been bypassed, ignored or insulted. Their self-centered nature is accompanied by grandiose projections of success. They do not want to feel dependent on or accountable to others, creating problems over their relationship to the board. A lack of empathy and, in the most extreme cases, lying, aggression and abuse are also features. An individual may also develop paranoid traits, convincing themselves that others, such as a board or rival leader or the business's owners, are out to get them. In contrast, top leaders who can express empathy, gratitude and acknowledge mistakes and failings and learn from them, tend to function at a higher level. They can correct errors, accept others' contributions and strategy formulation resulting in more stability and stronger decision making. Narcissism will be discussed further in Chapter 12, on psychodynamics.

5.6 Avoidance of Conflict

Succession developing into Shakespearian drama, as with Pimco, does not benefit anyone. And yet, for all the psychodrama on display and the costs to reputation and the bottom line, ultimately Pimco had continued to thrive under its Allianz ownership, at the time of writing. Gross, for all his eccentricities, had built a business that would outlive him. Gross claimed greed was a factor, but there was also a need to have, or replace, an iconic character.

Allianz's governing body allowed itself to be outmanoeuvred by the three lieutenants who threatened resignation. These three, and later a duo of two leaders, were for a while in charge of the leadership of Pimco. They would later be replaced with a single CEO. In psychological terms a way of "killing" a leader is often a threat and in the Pimco case, it was an initial alliance between three leaders that partook in this process in a destructive way. Such triumvirate leadership periods can last for longer or shorter time and usually with one partner as a buffer. In Pimco's case it was an uneasy balance between strong-willed leaders that was followed by an appointment of a new CEO after a few years. It illustrates the dynamic of "splitting", a very primitive defense mechanism where someone will be scapegoated or vilified in the process.

Conflict unresolved can lead to such avoidance of decisions and division within the board and in the leadership. Avoidance of mourning processes, lack of care of procedure that enables the drama of rivalry, envy and greed are very destructive. The brutal assassination of a leader, from the board or from inside the organization, is fuelled by strong emotions and will leave a void. Without a plan, and possibly exhausted or depleted by the preceding drama, further avoidance sets in. Over time such dynamics have been associated with political leadership as well as in family owed businesses. Box 5.1 shows how, after the assassination of Caesar, the senate was not effective and there was a long period of fragmentation and unstable alliances, which ultimately led to war.

BOX 5.1 OCTAVIAN BECOMING EMPEROR AUGUSTUS

By Agnes Wilhelmsen

Octavian was pronounced heir to Caesar in the dictator's will, presumably to Mark Antony's dismay. The years leading up to Caesar's assassination revolved around the senate heaping honors upon Caesar that he eagerly received. This led to Caesar assuming the role of dictator in perpetuity, a highly controversial and kingly position that counteracted the principles upon which the Republic was founded, principles that Brutus and Cassius no doubt had in mind leading up to the assassination. After

Cesar was killed Octavian, Lepidus and Antony form the second triumvirate in 43 BCE "legalized" under the Lex Titia. Instead of competing amongst themselves the triumvirate, none of whom liked or respected each other, was forged as they saw it would increase their chances of winning the civil war, the battle in Phillipi in 42 BCE, against the group of Caesar's assassins led by Brutus and Cassius. Like the first triumvirate, this political alliance dominated Roman politics and the three triumvirs no doubt found the political alliance advantageous.

However, Antony resented Octavian and spent much time campaigning in the east. Lepidus favored Antony but was (and felt like) a marginal figure in the trio. His presence nevertheless probably helped temper the tension between the two main rivals. Lepidus was eventually ejected out of the triumvirate and out of Rome. Antony became involved with Cleopatra, the Queen of Egypt, to the dismay of his wife, Octavia (Octavian's sister). Octavian stoutly retaining the title "triumvir" no doubt took this in his stride while acquiring popularity in Rome. Antony's residence in Egypt, his marriage to Cleopatra and his distribution of Roman territory to his children with Cleopatra became too much for Octavian and led to the Battle of Actium in 31 BCE. Antony and Cleopatra lost and later committed suicide. Octavian represents the righteous west and Antony the barbaric east, where Octavian prevails. As we see then Octavian's defeat of Antony emerges righteous, preoccupied with upholding the republican constitution and Roman values as seen in the (rather idealized) polarized position.

When Antony committed suicide Lapidus was also not a power factor and Octavian strives to restore the Republic after years of triumvirates, civil wars and general socio-political disarray. Octavian gave full power back to the senate, which had been disrupted by the triumvirate or civil war. He relinquished his provinces to the senate. Octavian acquired a vast fortune and wide recognition through Caesar's will, the civil war and his triple triumph in 29 BCE. The successive triumphs celebrated his three victories: Illyricum, Battle of Actium and conquest in Egypt. Octavian attempts in his Res Gestae (an autobiography) to downplay the civil quality in the Battle of Actium by categorizing it among his foreign victories where Antony becomes another eastern enemy.

Octavian was given the name Augustus (revered one) drawing from the religious realm rather than the political. He took on the title *Princeps*, however, as it emphasized his role as first among equals, hence the Principate, a role all succeeding emperors would assume as part of their integration in the Republican constitution. He took on the role of Pontifex Maximus although respectfully waited until Lepidus' death in 13 BCE to do so. This priesthood became an imperial privilege and lost its historical power. An alter of Peace, Ara Pacis, was commissioned and consecrated in 14BCE when Augustus returned from Hispania and was set up on the Campus Martius for all to see. A richly allusive and elaborate alter that was decorated with images of fertility and abundance, this hailed Augustus' Principate as a return to the golden age. This is known as the Pax Romana. The altar is beautifully ornate, interweaving Roman legend and deities, and republican values with Augustus and his family to further legitimize and consolidate their sovereignty over Rome and its empire.

Source: Alamy

Practice Summary

Duty of Care

The previous chapter on group dynamics together with this chapter on emotions form the basis for understanding the emotional and irrational dynamics that can obstruct the formulation of good succession strategies. As such the board has a duty to care about them. A board can create a list of checking points on the subject, to assess if they have addressed this crucial dimension. An external review can include them as topics when interviewing or helping the board review the process.

Diagnosis: Loss, Mourning and Sadness

Most seasoned top leaders have some experience in understanding such emotional reactions. In particular loss, mourning and sadness have a major impact and, unless one has had an exceptional life, one has encountered this oneself, or through other close friends and family. It is painful and therefore one tends to be sensitive in raising it as an issue. When in the role of securing or preparing for a succession one cannot take the risk of failing to address it, owing to its sensitivity. Helping an exiting CEO to address this might fall to the chair of the board.

Hope

Most leaders will recognize the motivating intent through the creation of new strategies and renewal. I describe this as hope, as it is an emotional state of curiosity, some excitement and what leaders try to evoke when they seek followership through visions and renewal. For it to be possible for a group to come along there is a need to address mourning and, if possible, give space for it to take place. Do not underestimate the effect of some informal, even if only fleeting, conversations. They can give the acknowledgment necessary for employees or leaders to create space for their private discussion, and addressing the issues that most affect them. With appropriate mourning, the mind will start other emotional processes that are necessary for being motivated and energetic about the future. The sadness experienced relates to the past, but when acknowledged it forms part of a process that will eventually generate a capability for moving on. This is the foundation for new hope and exploring new options and choices that can be relevant for decisions about the future. An exiting leader can set aside time in private, with close friends, colleagues or family members. The chair may have a role where there is a relationship of trust with the CEO, but this is not appropriate with an involuntary departure.

Narcissism and Hubris

An independent board, where the chair balances the power of the CEO, will be able to judge if the CEO is psychologically fit to be in the role. Within this realm, an overly narcissistic leader will have problems with accepting limitations to the executive authority that is given and ideally reviewed in a succession process. With regards to top leaders, there is a possibility that narcissism develops during the tenure. The board and chair will need to be willing to act strongly to curb it and limit the progression, otherwise it can become quite destructive. The judgment of whether a leader is too narcissistic and not fit for the job is not always straightforward, and consultation with clinically trained coaches or psychologists is recommended. During my career, both as a clinically trained psychologist and as a coach for top leaders, I have come across situations where someone is labelled a psychopath or narcissist from employees or other leaders. This is not adequate as a diagnosis.

References

Bowlby, J. (1980). *Attachment and loss: Separation: Anxiety and anger* (Vol. 2). Vintage.

Grady, J., Grady, V., McCreesh, P., & Noakes, I. (2019). *Workplace attachments: Managing beneath the surface.* Routledge.

Osnes, G. (Ed.). (2016). *Family capitalism: Best practices in ownership and leadership.* Taylor & Francis.

Panksepp, J., & Biven, L. (2012). *The archaeology of mind: Neuroevolutionary origins of human emotions.* WW Norton & Company.

Solms, M. (2015). *The feeling brain: Selected papers on neuropsychoanalysis.* Karnac Books.

6

LOGIC ON LEADERSHIP: HOW SUCCESSIONS CREATE LEADERSHIP

> Studying succession effectively is very close to understanding leadership.
>
> (Ocasio, 1999)

A succession process answers the question: with what authority? It is a question that goes beyond the personal authority one has developed over one's career and refers to how one was given authority that comes with the role one is in. For any leadership role there is a cultural and organizational aspect that does not have much to do with the actual leader. Most of us will, through films or real life experiences, have been exposed to or involved with very different organizations that we ourselves are familiar with and understand. Further, we are unavoidably involved in groups and organizations in different capacities: employee or leader, member, minority shareholder in a friend's suddenly hugely successful business, alumni from an educational organization, parent of a child attending school. We move in and out of our memberships with a plurality of logics of leadership and succession systems. This is most acute for top leaders working across cultures and in different types of organizations such as state departments, family-owned businesses and corporations or partnership structures. We often take for granted, or do not think about, with what authority these organizations are led. Only in crises, such as if a board is not able to create a succession outcome, might this question arise.

What one is confronted with is that leadership is also a cultural practice. Even within one region or country there will be subcultures. Importantly, there are different types of organizations that have enshrined logic in them on what will bring authority and followership. An example is religious organizations and tribes; they have a purpose that makes them have other logics on leadership than a family owed company or a business listed on the stock market. The difference between the two latter is often discussed as difference in governance, culture and/or values. What I suggest here captures where these different governing structures have one mutual converging aspect. Governing systems can be described according to their main function or task: to ensure good leadership. The purpose of the group or organization (including stakeholders) creates a strategy of norms and values for authority. These norms and values are enshrined into a leadership logic that is harboured in a succession system. The governing structure is designed so that it can manage the succession system and by this the leadership logic.

In this chapter I will show how leadership logics can be very different between different types of organizations. Some have one main type, such as elected leadership, that would be seen as strange for an outsider from the business world. Within a type of organization, such as publicly listed companies or a family-owned business, there will also be big differences that reflect the history, sector and culture. I will first describe a case where one of the controversies was whether there should be a change in leadership logic when a new CEO was appointed. The case is from Norway and the succession process in what is the biggest sovereign fund in the world, Norwegian Bank's Investment Management (NBIM).

I will also use three unusual organizations: the Vatican, tribe succession and Mossad. They will in different ways show leadership logics are maintained or changed in a succession. When they are changed a succession will trigger even more emotions and group processes than otherwise would be the case. This shows that if the purpose for an organization changes, or even is just slightly altered, often involving new or a change of stakeholders, an adaption or radical change in the leadership logic becomes a part of the succession process. Lastly I discuss how unconscious bias with regards to male and female authority affects leadership logics and succession.

The use of unusual cases should make it easier for readers to decode what leadership logic one has in organizations one is very familiar with. For myself, exposure to such a different type of organization was when I studied succession in tribes in Zimbabawe. With a high degree of diffe-rence between the cultures and types of systems, as a wider term than organizations, I had to take a step back and detach myself from what I had taken for granted with regards to certain assumptions. At that time I also worked as advisor and coach with a governance and succession process at a university in Norway and a family business in the UK. In both these latter cases, as in the main tribe I studied in Zimbabwe, the succession was disruptive for reasons that were hard to capture. Understanding the significance of leadership logics and the disruption in changing them made it possible to identify how some successions are so complex. It also allows for telling a story about the succession that in a concrete way shows how the organization is evolving and the succession often is a milestone in this process.

6.1 Legitimate Leadership and NBIM

A succession process at NBIM in 2020 shows how what could have been a relatively uncomplicated succession process became very controversial and publicly debated. A part of the problem was how an over-confident and conflict-avoiding chair and nomination committee did not follow the procedures established. Such procedures and rules always reflect important values and are important in building trust. In itself this was careless because it was a succession process in recruiting the new CEO of the world's biggest sovereign fund. NBIM is the biggest owner overall in the world and manages Norway's accumulated oil wealth abroad. It was a planned succession as the former CEO, Yngve Slyngstad, was leaving after 11 successful years in the role. The NBIM board, led by the CEO of the Norges Bank (Federal National Bank), set down a nomination committee of three people and by this excluded union representatives who by law should have been included. In itself such union representation is normal in Germany and Scandinavia and seen as unproblematic. Both Norges Bank and NBIM have independence but are also linked to and a part of governance rules for public institutions. Some of the bank's carelessness was in not having a correct public short list as the candidate they would offer the job, Nicolay Tangen, was not included.

They did not interview any of the internal candidates, which is always a bad practice even though one might know that none of them would be seen as up for the role. It later emerged that one of the internal candidates was regarded as a good choice but still not interviewed.

Before describing other aspects this case, I want to emphasize that no one in any way suggested that Nicolay Tangen did not have outstanding results and capacities for the role he would get in the end. He had built up his own company as fund manager in London. The mistakes were twofold and the reactions fed into each other; one on procedure and one on logic on leadership. The procedural mistakes were surprisingly naive: unfortunate exclusion or lack of transparency into the succession pool and short list, no clarity on who should be presented in the nomination committee and, further, the integrity of those on that committee. Tangen had, as a wealthy man, sponsored and invited members of the Norwegian elite to luxurious trips in the USA with private planes and celebrity concerts and some of the members of the committee had partaken in these. A certain context is necessary with regards to the procedural mistakes; Norway is a highly egalitarian society and in addition Tangen lived, for tax reasons, in London. He would put his own wealth in a blind trust but still would not solve issues around his wealth and legal status. NBIM has as a global investor developed a role where they demand a place at the nomination committees of the companies they are the second-biggest owner of. There is also an explicit policy of the fund, intended to limit the risk they can take, to be active in promoting good governance practices in the companies they have big investments in. If a new CEO himself had been recruited in a way not representing such best practices for the organization there would be an issue around trustworthiness.

One could say that this is problematic and unnecessary and one could weather the public criticism and scrutiny. Another more deep-seated issue is at stake and might also reflect the carelessness of the Chair of the nomination committee. It is a question about the evolution of NBIM and what it represents. Slyngstad was the second CEO of the organization. Over this tenure the fund, due to the increase of income from oil and down payment of debt developing this sector, had increased exponentially and in 2019 it passed the value of $10 trillion. Over the last 5–10 years the government had imposed certain restrictions on how they could invest that also had a political agenda. NBIM was leading in not investing in the tobacco or weapons industries. The political agenda would include global warming and sustainability leadership. The fund had disinvested in the fossil fuel sector. It also had meetings with companies on their tax location if it was seen that it was an avoidance tax plan.

Shifting Leadership Logic

A leadership logic is an attempt to create a rational basis, and expression of some values and norm, for what the role will represent. Many within the business community will identify, and have the most trust in, a merit-based succession system. Family-owed or family-led businesses are in parts exceptions to this. The purpose of a family-owed company is often very long term – the hand over to the next generation. Due to the long-term perspective, often 20 to 30 years or more, a leadership logic will often be that the business is controlled or led by family members that also will hand over founder, or business, values, seen to reflect past success. Increasingly, business skills and experience outside the family business are seen as part of the necessary logic for trust. For a family-owed business certain idiosyncratic values such as involvement with local community, risk taking, new entrepreneurship, patient capital or low revenues might be used.

As with NBIM the logic of leadership for the first CEO tenure is to establish a new organization that has complex governance and stakeholder issues. For the second CEO, Slyngstad, it was to manage the growth of assets and an increasing global visibility and significance of the fund. The third CEO tenure, with the fall in oil prices and consequent expected fall in revenue, sustainability movement, a recession and high state debt, some would argue that the role would now be more progressive and more a role of social leadership. It was argued that one should have the best traders but not necessarily be led by one. In addition one would have a progressive political role on the world stage and it would be legitimate, as many did, to argue that an added purpose would lead to a need to change the leadership logic for the top leadership. One of the troubles with not following the procedures was that certain possible difficult discussions on the leadership logic were avoided. Taking for granted that the old leadership logic would prevail without debate, also called groupthink, made the chair of the nomination committee completely unprepared for a long and heated public and political debate. Had the procedures been followed one would have had wider representation, such as union representatives, and a broader discussion on what the next leader would represent. The succession outcome would most likely have been the same but one would have been prepared, and could have articulated and argued, for the choices. All these aspects are part of the process of creating trust and legitimacy. Still, even if all the other aspects of a succession are done right, the logic on leadership and how it is discussed would be the first and crucial step that can derail a succession process.

Below are some more unusual cases of the types of succession systems and logic for leadership. As we are heading into a more complex business and economic world these unusual cases show how there are many options to be inspired by when one develops possible new ways of thinking about leadership. We are facing disruptions such as sustainability leadership and global warming, Artificial Intelligence, a global and national recession and possibly a long period of high employment among young people and it is hard to predict how, and to what, old and new organizations will adapt. An additional argument for selecting unconventional examples for a business book is to prompt reflection on our use of metaphors – for example, phrases like "fight for the throne" can appear in the succession process. In other cultures groups such as tribes, religious organizations and security organizations might be more important, both in real life and as metaphors or references points, for how things are governed and what leadership is.

6.2 The Vatican

The Catholic Church is perhaps the institution in the world with the longest historical record of leadership successions, dating back centuries. When the conclave has decided upon a new Pope, white smoke emerges from the chimney of the Sistine Chapel and the announcement "Habemos Papa" is made. It is of importance for millions of people across the world, who look to the church for spiritual guidance. In addition to millions of followers it is also an institution that organizes not-for-profit humanitarian efforts. The hierarchical and patriarchal nature of the institution has come under justified criticism, especially over the cover-ups of scandals concerning the sexual abuse of children.

The Vatican has favoured a strong element of continuity through the succession from one Pope to the next. There may be a change in emphasis, such as with the liberal Pope John XXIII in 1958 and more recently with the current Pope Francis, or a conservative such as Pope John-Paul II in 1978. An overwhelming emphasis upon continuity has also included steps of progression. These forces are currently, after the current Pope decided to name himself after the philanthropic Saint Francis, a focus on the poor and "ministry", in contrast to what he sees as pomp and decadence.

As a succession system it is largely unchanging and faithfully observed, with comparatively minor changes over the centuries. The design of the succession system specifies cardinals under 70 years of age as the pool of candidates from which to select the next Pope. A Pope will, during his tenure, replace cardinals who pass away, or can increase the number of cardinals and by this way influence future successions. A rule explicitly forbids discussion among the cardinals, or a decision to be made, before the conclave starts its work. The conclave's proceedings form a part of the succession system where discussion is combined with prayers, religious ceremonies and voting for candidates. The proceedings are specifically designed, with prayers, so as to allow the Holy Spirit to intervene. Such a leadership logic ensures that the Pope will symbolize divine authority. With the Holy Spirit's intervention the succession system harbours the logic that the Pope will, for a member of the Church, be God's divine authority on Earth.

6.3 Tribe Successions

For my research, I was keen to supplement studies of succession in Western organizations with observations of how the process works in other settings. In Middle Eastern and African traditions, the concept of ownership of land was alien before the age of colonization. Many groups were nomadic and still are throughout the Middle East and Africa. Tribes and clans were more fluid; traditionally the tribe might have effective sovereignty over an area of land but not private ownership as we know it. Among a tribal chief's responsibilities was to grant rights to use of land and settle disputes. A leader could be deposed if he was corrupt, or otherwise not able to protect and provide for the tribe's needs.

In Saudi Arabia, as in many African tribes, a brother-to-brother succession system, also known as agnatic seniority, had been in place. This has been the case in the ruling family of Saud, since the dynasty was founded by Ibn Saud (1875–1953). The succession from the founder went to his oldest son and, through a brother-to brother succession system, through six brothers.

In tribe succession, when the brother has deceased, the descendants of each brother would be a "house", and the succession would move from house to house in the birth order of the founder's sons. Mohammed bin Salman, currently Crown Prince of Saudi Arabia, was in 2017 anointed by his father as the successor, replacing his older cousin Mohammad bin Nayef as both Crown Prince and heir. Many of the strong man actions attributed to the new Crown Prince most likely relate to how he has to force the other houses of the Saudi tribe to accept the shift that started in 2017/2018. Each branch has lost their right, when a King dies, to elect a successor from their extensive family. It is a complicated system also due to polygamy, and brothers with inheritance rights include the "Sudairi Seven". Sudairi was Ibn Saud's favourite wife and, as the biggest sibling group, they managed to keep the succession between themselves.

Many succession systems in all cultures involve symbolic rituals of little obvious practical utility, but which nonetheless do serve a purpose in conveying a message to the successor and the wider population that the values and the institution are being safeguarded. In the Shona tribe in Zimbabwe a chief could not name a successor directly, but instead indicated a candidate by delegating tasks belonging to the role. After a chief died or was deposed the tribe would collectively discuss and choose a new chief, in many tribes with a consensus process rather than a vote. A clan or tribe had therefore, as in Saudi Arabia, freedom of choice in selecting a successor among different contenders. If the candidate fell short in these factors, the bloodline or seniority would be disregarded. In this way some sense of meritocracy was honored (Osnes, 2011).

6.4 Logics on Leadership in Mossad

Another different, but revealing, case of succession is drawn from an Israeli security organization. In particular it illustrates how important the succession pool is as a strategy, but also how this is just part of the dynamic. Israel has several security spy and counterterrorist organizations. There is a widespread belief, across the political spectrum, that these organizations are essential in securing the very survival of Israel. The succession system and pool of candidates are determined by a policy where all employees have to leave the organization when they are 45 years old. Former employees and leaders will receive a small pension for the rest of their lives. The pension expense matches the significance it accords these types of organizations.

Employees and leaders can apply for an exemption and stay until they are 50 years old. As a consequence all top leaders including the most senior will be 50 years old or younger.

The entry into the security organization starts with conscription into the armed forces. With men and women conscripted, the security organizations can screen almost the whole population for the brightest or fittest for such work. Military service is relatively long both for men and women and it creates strong ties among them. When they leave in their mid to late 40s, former army friends constitute a social network that provides new employment, a compensation for the financial and professional sacrifice in what is generally a low paid occupation, despite a life-long pension, in a role to defend the country.

Through such a succession pool strategy there is a balance between experience and ruthless innovation, almost at any cost. One obvious objective is to retain and motivate bright people within the service. A retirement age of 45 to 50 is seen to balance experience in the leaders with new ideas and innovative thinking in the top leadership team. This was expressed to me as: "Overall – we have found that when everyone leaves at 45 years old, or possibly a few years later as top leader, we are balancing on a tipping point where we stay innovative, innovating but also possess enough experience."

Internationally Israel security organizations have a reputation of being very disciplined and ruthless. They are assumed responsible for the assassination of enemies posing a direct threat to the Israeli state, such as a leader of the Hamas terrorist organization, or a nuclear scientist in Iran; attributions that are neither officially confirmed nor denied. While the Israeli security organizations also have a high proportion of women, probably the highest of the world's security services, one is left to speculate what the early retirement age does to an organization where relatively young men, with correspondingly high levels of testosterone, are at the top of the organization. Testosterone is one of the hormones and neurotransmitters in the brain that, in addition to male sexual desire, promotes aggressive behaviour specifically when personal space is threatened.

6.5 Gender Bias

Debate will probably always continue among historians as to whether highly influential individuals, the Great Man theory, or wider social and environmental developments have the dominant influence on major events.

What research does confirm is that *belief* in the Great Man theory has been significant. One simple study at Colombia University Business School in New York invited participants divided into two groups to appraise the identical resumes respectively of Howard and Heidi. The Heidi Roizen profile originated in a successful Silicon Valley venture capitalist. Professor Frank Flynn used the profile and CV and presented half his class with it using Heidi's name, while the other half was given the exact same case study but with the name Howard. The students rated Howard and Heidi equally competent, but they liked Howard, but not Heidi. Those assessing Howard's CV praised him as strong and effective, and someone they would like to work for.

The group assessing Heidi's also rated her as accomplished, but commented that she came across as selfish and that they would be less eager to work for her.

Unconscious gender-related biases are a type of cognitive bias where our perception of certain characteristics and competences in male and female leaders are formed irrespective of their effectiveness. While a female leader may receive positive feedback on being clear, strategic and goal-orientated, she is also more likely to be perceived as pushy or aggressive in doing so (Eagly and Karau, 2002).

Diversity initiatives have sometimes been inadequate, resulting in women being promoted with little preparation, or given near-impossible roles – the so-called glass cliff. A white male elite preserving their own entitlement, most likely unwittingly, is currently shifting in some industries and sectors. Making such unconscious biases conscious demands some effort, either through regulation or in challenging one's own bias. Not only do men keep the glass ceiling in place, women participate, again unwittingly. Talented women may face two fronts to protect themselves: from men feeling threatened in their hierarchies and sometimes female rivalry and a sense of sisterly betrayal. Women organize their social groups less hierarchically and might resent a break from the more equal distribution of power. In Box 6.1 I will refer to two films that show unconscious bias against strong female leadership, and the eventual pushback from the leader Anna Wintour, the legendary editor of *Vogue* magazine. In the image she is, famously, with dark glasses awaiting a fashion show, hiding her well-acknowledged "editing eye".

BOX 6.1 *THE DEVIL WEARS PRADA*

The film *The Devil Wears Prada* came out in 2006. It is based on a book with the same name, written by one of the female assistants of Anna Wintour. It had a male director, but female producer and screenwriter. Meryl Streep played Wintour. The film does not directly name Wintour – the lead character is called Miranda Priestly – but the references are clear; Prada is known to be Wintour's favourite fashion brand. The backdrop for the story is how the assistant suffers from Wintour's whims and difficult demands, for example having to pick up her coffee with very specific demands, get first editions of Harry Potter books and so on. One is left to muse over the possibility of whether a male top leader many of us have worked for would have been ridiculed and critiqued as a devil for displaying such whims. Top leaders of any gender can develop neurotic habits, and the ones displayed by the Wintour character are low on the scale by any measure; certainly not a case of bullying or abuse. Male leaders have such idiosyncrasies celebrated as indicators of maverick genius. What is not in focus in the film in how Anna Wintour, a strong leader for 20 years in her role as fashion editor of *Vogue* New York, has been the undisputed fashion trendsetter in the world. She and her team maintained *Vogue* as the most important fashion outlet, with her at the helm with the best "editing eye" in fashion. She helped identify and encourage new styles, and also new stars. Her influence was considerable; the way in which top fashion houses edit and design determines what high street and cheaper brands will produce by way of imitation. The logic on how a woman can be punished for being a strong leader, as shown in the Heidi/Howard experiment, is vividly illustrated.

Anna Wintour's response was subtle. In 2007, while her team was creating what is the most important issue of a year for *Vogue*, the September edition, gave full access to a documentary team to make a film about the creative effort. "The September Issue", a film released in 2009, shows the work, and her leadership, in a balanced way, not confined to flattering scenes. Wintour appears unapologetic and the film shows the stress and tensions involved in creative team effort: costs, innovation, financial profit, advertisers, risk and uncertainty. Grace Coddington, former model turned creative director and who dares to stand up to Anna Wintour, is shown as creative and with complementary talents. This is significant, because Coddington has often been portrayed as the leading victim of Wintour's strong leadership. The relationship between Wintour and

Coddington is complex, as it always is within leadership duos and teams. Wintour recognizes Coddington's expertise and keen eye for design. The image shows the pair, Wintour famously behind dark glasses, awaiting a fashion show.

Source: Alamy

Unconscious bias about the individual masculine nature of leadership has had a distorting effect on our understanding of how businesses are founded, developed and sustained, and how authority is transferred in a succession. Much traditional business education and theory has focused on the individual as the sole source of leadership. In earlier family business literature, the contribution of women as co-entrepreneurs was often neglected, both in informal leadership roles and within the family (Barrett & Moores, 2009). Newer research confirms that women frequently take on significant leading roles, as active owners or otherwise in strategic positions (Karataş-Özkan et al., 2011).

Resonating with the Heidi/Howard experiment a notion of the Great Man theory on leadership has focused on how we culturally identify certain male personality traits as being synonymous with leadership. In reality, an individual executive may thrive in one context but struggle in another, and leadership relies on collaboration, culture and the ongoing establishment of trust. A further distortion has been created by the emphasis in recent decades on managing to meet short-term targets for shareholder value, an approach that has come under criticism for encouraging opportunistic executives to game the system, or neglect resilience in pursuit of short-term headline profits.

Practice Summary

There is a general acknowledgement within the research field that successions are linked to the type of institutions they occur in. It is a process that defines what is seen as legitimate authority and has within the field been regarded as the missing link between successions and how it shapes leadership. I suggest that the "stake" in a succession is how the leader represents a value or norm derived from a purpose and its stakeholders. A succession is in this way also a symbolic event.

Cultural Understanding

Many top leaders will, over a long career, exit and enter into several different types of organizations and possibly cultures. All succession processes will, unwittingly or not, involve the development of strategies for each practice, involving substantial effort on behalf of decision makers, and will be unique to the organization. They will differ between cultures and relate to the challenges of the organization, based on how successions involve the seven different strategy practices and how the development of strategy is contingent on the type of organization, organizational challenges and culture. To be able to see the top leadership processes with a perspective of understanding the unique features of how an organization has defined leadership is important.

Understanding Legitimacy

The legitimacy of the leadership succession process and leadership logic are intimately linked with each other, and the two are mutually supportive. An inability to strategize a leadership succession would ultimately delegitimize the governing structure. Indeed, such failure can have wider implications, weakening trust in the organization in employees, shareholders, regulators, customers and the wider public. It might be that the succession system itself, and the leadership logic it is meant to preserve, will have to change. Such a radical succession will often be dramatic and complex to manage. Such a transformation will be described more in detail in Chapter 8; how an externally recruited leader can be challenged in entering into a role when the succession system and logic of leadership have been changed.

This chapter has dealt with the context from a cultural point of view. The logic of leadership for each institution has to suit its unique culture: both internal culture, and that of the society in which it operates. The succession system reveals how culture, at an operational level, shapes leadership. There can be cultural differences across nations and continents and different institutions within one region. Important to many organizations, especially those that are long-lasting and with a strong sense of purpose, are rituals that symbolize the continuity of shared values. Seemingly redundant and odd practices that take place during a succession hold much symbolic meaning to members, holding the group together and enhancing a sense of safety.

References

Barrett, M., & Moores, K. (2009). *Women in family business leadership roles.* Edward Elgar Publishing.

Eagly, A. H., & Karau, S. J. (2002). Role congruity theory of prejudice towards female leaders. *Psychological Review, 109*(3), 573–598.

Giambatista, R. C., Rowe, W. G., & Riaz, S. (2005, p. 966). Nothing succeeds like succession: A critical review of leader succession literature since 1994, *The Leadership Quarterly, 16*(6), 963–991. doi:10.1016/j.leaqua.2005.09.005.

Karataş-Özkan, M., Erdogan, A., & Nicolopoulou, K. (2011). Women in Turkish family businesses: Drivers, contributions and challenges. *International Journal of Cross Cultural Management, 11*(2), 203–219. https://doi.org/10.1177/1470595811399189

Ocasio, W. (1999). Institutionalized action and corporate governance: The reliance on rules of CEO succession. *Administrative Science Quarterly*, 44(2), 384–416.

Osnes, G. (2011). Succession and authority: A case study of an African family business and a clan chief. *International Journal of Cross Cultural Management*, 11(2), 185–201.

PART II

ENTRY OF A CEO AND FOLLOWERSHIP

7

AGENT OF EVOLUTION OR TRANSFORMATION?

When a succession is in progress, employees, board members and other leaders begin by thinking about what they would like to see in the next leader. Increasingly stakeholders will request or push for a succession if they think the organization has stagnated. Instinctively it seems to trigger a judgement on the balance between continuity and change. With regards to succession, what will be expected of the new leader will be captured in a mandate, initially formulated as a first step in the process and with possible amendments throughout. The degree of specificity will be different and also be a process of a dialogue with candidates and the board. If not addressed explicitly it can compromise the effectiveness of the succession pool. Lack of agreement within a board or among owners can lead to different candidates representing different mandates; this in itself reduces the options if a mandate, however specific, has been determined beforehand. A mandate reflects expectations about the future, and whether it will be focused on continuity or change or a combination.

It is generally assumed that an external candidate is better positioned to be the agent of radical changes than an internal one. There is little real evidence to support this, however – it is more of an assumption. There is no consistent finding that an external CEO generally does better than an internally recruited one. Given the complex interactions of individual and team performance, this finding is hardly surprising. It is not only the top leader who determines performance. Other key experts, key leaders or sales efforts are also significant, while external events such as disruptive competitors can have a big effect. In some sectors, new products and services take many years to develop, so a new leader may inherit the benefits of much earlier investment or, conversely, have to face the challenge of a prior failure to invest. Taking all such factors into account is an important part of the evaluation of top leaders when assessing them. Some leadership tenures are exceptions such as saving an organization from a crisis and immediate demise. On a long-term basis the assessment is about the leader's capability to develop individuals, teams and systems and create value. From a research point of view, the multiple variables that affect performance are such that valid research findings have proved elusive when trying to assess the effectiveness of internal versus external candidates (e.g. Giambatista et al., 2005).

This chapter will explore a well documented case, HSBC and its latest CEO succession process of summer 2019. It would have the potential of being a disruptive succession. The HSBC case sets the stage for discussing aspects of the debate, or choice, between recruiting a new CEO from outside or inside of the organization. Following sections discuss the overlap between the HR strategies and the succession strategies at the board level. This chapter aims to guide a board, chair, top leaders and the organization in how to discuss the overlap and to communicate some of the issues it raises within the organization. Such a collaboration can be a crucial preparation in the hand over process (see Chapter 8). The significance of a mandate for evolution, change or radical change and transformation is discussed.

Disruptive Successions

With today's increasing turbulence due to competition in markets, the sustainability movement, political risk, technological innovation and disruption, the notion of continuity as a stable organization with unchanged identity is an illusion. I have replaced it with the notion of evolution, where small step changes at least are necessary, and sometimes more radical change. Major change, for example to turn around a financially perilous situation or transform a culture, can become a process of identity transformation. Often, but not necessarily, organizations try to implement it through a change in leadership. Shorter CEO tenures have been attributed to a high degree of turbulence and disruption.

On entry as a CEO one can be the change agent for a shift in leadership logic that can have caused, or will cause, a loss process. Such an emotional reaction can be unsettling through the organization and sometimes one idealizes a former leader that came to symbolize such a logic. A change in leadership logic can be resisted by the upper echelon or a broader elite and can lead to attempts to oust or scapegoat a new leader. These topics are covered in the earlier chapters. In the last section in this chapter I discuss how the entry process also must be seen as entry onto a stage of symbolic leadership. A leadership logic will exclude and include certain candidates into the succession pool and by this be a process of identity formation for the organization. In that regard what is excluded is put into the shadow of "things not done here". The last chapter will address organization shadows and its implication for a succession process and the collaboration between the board, CEO and organization. The amount of changes, and internally or externally recruited CEO, will be processes influencing the entry of a new CEO and the handover process and this is described in this chapter.

7.1 HSBC and the First Outsider CEO

The Chair of the Board of HSBC, Mark Tucker, in August 2019, surprised the corporate world when he ousted the CEO John Flint just 18 months after Flint's appointment. Tucker was the first external appointment chair of the board and he himself had appointed Flint in February 2018. The business and reputational risk were considerable. HSBC is a large financial institution employing over 200,000 people and has, since it was founded as the Hong Kong & Shanghai Bank in the 1850s, only recruited from their internal leadership pool to the most senior executive position. One insider told a journalist that Tucker wanted more aggressive cost-cutting and ambitious targets for profits (Chatterjee and White, 2019). What was clear was that a desired strategic change prompted a succession and that this shift would include something of a culture change too.

Opening up the CEO post to external candidates sent ripples through the corporate world and among the bank's own employees. The aim appeared to be based on a desire to turn around the bank's fortunes in the USA and usher in a more performance-focused approach, but these factors were generally not seen as obvious triggers for such a dramatic move. Corporate results, while not spectacular, were hardly a failure either. Traditional succession planning had focused on developing internal candidates for the role. The strategy was based on a notion that the bank was so complex that only an insider could understand the complexity of a bank covering all continents with complex services and structures, and a proud culture. In Hong Kong the bank was seen as so powerful that when its leader, based in Hong Kong, retired he would move from the island, owing to an issue of casting a shadow/legacy. HSBC grew from the Hong Kong & Shanghai Bank and expanded significantly into the UK market with the takeover of the Midland Bank in 1992, a bank which, despite its name, was not regional but was one of the biggest nationwide banks at the time. The Midland brand was discontinued in 1999. Around 80% of the bank's profits, nonetheless, were in Asian markets at the time of writing.

With a relatively new chair of board and new CEO, both recruited from outside the organization, one is departing from a central part of the bank's narrative, which said that "We breed our own leaders". That is not a minor change. The challenges for an incoming CEO, whether internal or external, might be considerable. Some of the questions that are raised concern important questions around the role of the chair, the CEO–chair relationship, the internal reaction and development of leaders generally within the bank.

Immediately after the ousting of Flint speculation arose among employees, and in the business press, as to whether Tucker would take over as the de facto strategic leader himself. Many of the questions that arose are typical of the inside/outside discussion with regards to recruitment of CEOs. What would someone from the outside, at least in the HSBC context, imply in terms of the level of followership of a new leader? What type of welcome and what type of followership? Will there be resentment from internal candidates where a sense of entitlement, and ambitions, have been frustrated? What happens within an internal talent pool of potential leaders, a possible brain-drain? What about the frustration where career choices have been based on a succession tradition of internal promotion? At the time of writing, it was set to be an interesting CEO entry.

7.2 Inside or Outside Recruitment

Changes in employment patterns have altered the perception of external candidates, and what they represent. The practice of staying with one employer for life is no longer common. It is not necessarily seen as a betrayal to leave and work for another company, even a competitor, after being considered part of the pool identified for promotion. In one complex succession on which I advised, a former leader, after seven years of outside leadership experience, returned as the new CEO. Such a trajectory and recruitment is unusual but shows ingenuity. It also combines the pros and cons of recruiting from inside the organization or from outside.

Sometimes a board might choose to recruit a high-profile external leader as a symbolic gesture so as to indicate change. Whether radical change of the kind that is desired will actually occur is another issue. If the decision is only at the symbolic level, there may be a lack of definition and communication of the desired change, or lack of a strong enough mandate for change. While there might be good arguments for recruiting an external CEO, it can be demotivating for potential leaders in the company's own pipeline. They may cease to consider the internal leadership trajectory as their preferred career path, and seek a top leadership role somewhere else. It can lead to a depletion of talent. Many companies also have pride in being able to train their own leaders. This can be a strength, but there can also be benefits from experience in other organizations. Some excellent family business owners encourage family members intended for top leadership roles to gain external experience.

The inside/outside debate is therefore more complex than a choice of continuity versus change, or a question of loyalty. Several considerations need to be taken into account. The decision hinges more on how clear a mandate for a new leader is, and what type. A clear mandate for change can empower a suitably qualified internal candidate to oversee radical transformation, with the benefit that they know the organization well. An outsider will, by necessity, have to learn the culture and ways of working, and may be less precise in their identification of necessary reforms. They will be free from close personal relationships, which offers both advantages and disadvantages. There will be less leverage from strong bonds of loyalty, but at the same time they will not be identified with certain internal groups, or identified with an aspect of the organization's legacy. External reviews, and assessment of both internal and external candidates by headhunters, can be invaluable for a board.

7.3 Internal Talent Pool

Major companies, such as the oil giants, many financial companies like HSBC and conglomerates like the GE led by Jack Welch in the late 20th Century, have a long tradition of investing heavily in development of internal leadership talent. They become academy companies, with extensive inhouse training. The investment is significant, and it can be difficult to assess returns, or to benchmark against external leadership candidates. The practice develops a potentially strong internal resource. It also requires sensitive handling, as it also builds up expectations, and talented leaders can be attractive to rival companies. Such an HR policy is highly relevant to the issue of succession to the top leadership role. It addresses a resource dependency on talent, or the "war on talent", coined by McKinsey, and ensuring an internal talent pool can be a part of succession planning that the board can choose to invest in. Moreover, it can help maintain and nurture the organization's values. As it lies within the company's control, it can be used to improve diversity in leadership roles.

Leadership development programmes often form part of comprehensive talent development and assessment programmes run by the HR department and whether the board should have a role in such internal processes is disputed. Some argue a board should treat internal leadership training, or talent management, as an ongoing discipline. A board, more than the CEO, will consider future as well as current leadership needs, in some cases preparing for more diversity – in leadership styles as well as diversity in terms of background. It can be helpful to have a board member nominated with responsibility for overseeing leadership talent, internally and externally, for both current and future needs.

Leadership training practices have also changed. Working in partnership with external coaches and a business school rather than creating an internal teaching faculty is growing in popularity. Using external coaches can be of assistance in terms of ensuring confidentiality. The discussion and evaluation of the usefulness, and effectiveness, of leadership training is a field in itself. It is beyond the scope of this book to make any firm conclusion beyond showing that it will be a part of the succession strategy to determine if one is to have such programmes. Whatever position one has, there will be implications for the entry process of a new CEO. The returns of internal leadership development programmes may be difficult to assess. Leaders one has invested in might leave for other roles, yet again, one might recruit a leader someone else has trained. One illustration of the dynamic concentrated learning situations can have on creating leadership is shown in Box 7.1, a rather sinister example. It shows the extent to which prisons have unintentionally become leadership training programmes for terrorist organizations and criminal gangs.

BOX 7.1 INCUBATION OF DEADLY LEADERSHIP

The leader of the Islamic State (ISIS) or Daesh, Baghdadi – whose real name was Ibrahim Awwad Ibrahim al-Badri (1971–2019) – was born into a religious Sunni Arab family claiming their ancestors from the Prophet Muhammad's Quraysh tribe; by this he possessed one of the key qualifications of becoming a caliph, or leader. At its peak between 2014 and 2016, Islamic State controlled 88,000 sq km (34,000 sq miles) of territory in western Syria and eastern Iraq, imposing a savage regime on eight million people. It was a brutal rule that included killings of political competitors and members of other religious groups, and systemic rape of women. ISIS generated billions of dollars of revenue from oil, extortion and kidnapping. It pillaged and ruined invaluable cultural artefacts.

The crucible for Islamic State was a prison run by the USA armed forces following their overthrow of the Saddam Hussein regime in Iraq in 2003/2004. In early 2004, Baghdadi established the social network and teachings that would be the basis for ISIS. Baghdadi were with a group, including some of Saddam Hussein's officers and Ba'ath Party members, detained by USA troops in Falluja. The detention centre at Camp Bucca became the incubator of him as a leader and a network of followers who were radicalized through dialogues and discussions. It is disputed how organized they were and most likely there were autonomous units all with a strong purpose. In Falluja Baghdadi led prayers, delivered sermons and gave religious classes to inmates, indoctrinating a corrupted form of Islamism, featuring extreme intolerance of all Western ideas. He later became, as a sort of chair, the head of ISIS Sharia committee. The incubation of ISIS, and training ground for future top leaders, took place under the noses of USA military guards.

After ten months Baghdadi was released as a low-threat prisoner. He came in contact with the al-Qaeda terrorist group led by Abu Musab al-Zarqawi. When Zarqawi was killed in a USA air strike in 2006, al-Qaeda changed its name to the Islamic State of Iraq (ISI). Baghdadi would lead ISI's Sharia committees and partake in its consultative Shura Council. With Saddam-era military and intelligence officers, among them fellow former Camp Bucca inmates, he built ISIS.

Source: *Alamy*

Similar types of imprisonment that have contributed to the incubation of new criminal ventures, training of leaders and development of networks and leadership structures have been documented more broadly. The HBO series *The Wire*, in the first season, showed how gang membership is one, if not the only, entrepreneurial type of work available to inner city Black men. Through imprisonment of narco-gang leaders, soldiers and middle managers socialize and exchange ideas and negotiate; they are trained and develop strategies, and establish a broader network.

7.4 Mandate and CEO Entry

Ignoring the formulation of a mandate in a succession can create a false sense of agreement on what the new leader's regime should be. There can be conflicting views and predictions, and expectations, that can make the entry of a CEO very difficult or impossible. A mandate might not be perfectly carved out prior to appointment, but there should be broad agreement on the essential elements. A new CEO must also be able to know what it is, more than a loose idea. In the best of conditions it should excite and challenge a leader. In preparation, or before accepting a CEO role, an incoming leader should try to mitigate such risk to the entry process, and possibly to their own career, and question and probe the board about their expectations. Equally serious is a partially formed mandate where the board has presented a veneer of unity, or a false agreement, that covers up divisions. This can lead to complications in direction and create the potential for serious problems in strategy formation and execution.

The best qualified leader available could fail if he or she is not well suited to the mandate; ensuring a good match is the responsibility of the board and the candidate alike. Several cases illustrate this risk; examples where a leader was selected to lead a process of transformation and radical change, only for the board to fail to support the new CEO once risk and turmoil followed. The new CEO may have been a good fit for the radical mandate, but the board was not. An incoming CEO should make sure of, and have a dialogue about, the authority and discretion given and how this is linked to the mandate. A previous leadership tenure may have failure rooted in problems at the board; giving too little authority and interfering too much, undermining the CEO. Leadership is contextual, so it can only be assessed by way of an understanding of the whole context: whether the governance is fit for purpose, the autonomy granted and the brief appropriate, and so on.

For the governing body, to maximize the chances of a successful succession, a superficial, individualistic approach needs replacing with multidimensional analysis. A new CEO who is entering a context where a former leader has been scapegoated is on uncertain ground. Scapegoating can become a slippery slope where a board, the chair or other top leader has managed to take some of ownership of previous failures. A focus on personal weaknesses of an individual leader is, most often, a version of history where institutional weaknesses are overlooked, combined with unreasonable expectations of the new leader (scapegoating is discussed at length in Chapter 4).

7.5 Entry onto the Stage of Symbolic Leadership

On the entry into a role as a top CEO one has to address, and know, if one is the agent of change or continuity and to what extent the succession included a change in the leadership logic. The question one has to address, as described in Chapter 6, is what authority and leadership logic is given to one as leader. While the leadership ahead will address strategic challenges and the needs of followers there is a system and cultural hand-over one needs to be aware of. This is in particular if there have been an institutional shift in the succession process.

To illustrate the symbolic aspect of taking up a top leadership role, and possibly how to decode and understand certain rituals, I include a story around Napoleon and a famous image of his ascension as Emperor (see Box 7.2). It accentuates a part of one's leadership and how one is, at any time, also on the stage. One's non-verbal cues, how one creates a setting or changes it, at the conscious or unconscious level, will be read and deciphered by stakeholders and employees. It is important that one's staging and symbolic performance is aligned with what the logic on leadership is, or is meant to be. Often it is more vaguely described as culture but this is a broad term. It is beneficial, in particular for the relationship between the CEO and the board, to clarify the logic of leadership and what expectations and assumptions there have been in the past and will be for the next tenure. Below is an analysis of Napoleon and how he communicated and maneuvered his stage and PR on his accession as Emperor.

BOX 7.2 NAPOLEON AND THE CRAVING FOR LEGITIMACY

By Agnes Wilhelmsen

Napoleon was an outstanding general born to minor Tuscan nobility in Corsica, in an Italian commune later transferred to France. He rose to power as an outsider, his armies conquered much of continental Europe and his reign was one of constant warfare. Given that the revolution created his route to power, and that many of his reforms were modernizing, imposing the Napoleonic code and fighting feudalism, there was a paradox in granting himself a flamboyant coronation in a cathedral with Papal approval. There are various points of comparison and contradiction encapsulated in this highly stylized Jacques-Louis David painting of Napoleon's coronation in 1807. One can perceive friction between military and royal authority, between tradition and controversy, between the private and the public, between social mobility and imperial grandeur. Less than 15 years after the last Bourbon king was executed in a violent revolution that heralded a secular republic, the ceremony is unmistakably regal, and Catholic.

Source: *Alamy*

Yet despite the traditional trappings, there are many unconventional aspects to the ceremony. Firstly, it is set at Notre Dame in Paris rather than the traditional setting at the Cathedral in Reims, opening up the sacred event to a more populist and political backdrop (in the following century, a similar move was made by the British House of Windsor when agreeing to the televising of Elizabeth II's coronation in 1953). Although the painting is called the "Coronation of Napoleon", we see here Napoleon already wreathed with a laurel crown and instead the focus is on his wife, Josephine, being crowned. Strategically it seems Jacques-Louis David focuses on the moment where Napoleon has taken the role of Pope Pius VII in crowning Josephine as Empress. Napoleon himself was crowned by Pope Pius VII but in the picture the crown is held by Napoleon in a manner that could be perceived as him crowning himself.

Apparently there are outlines in the painting of an earlier version, in which Napoleon was indeed crowning himself. A surviving sketch by

Jacques-Louis David at the Louvre Museum in Paris depicts this supremely narcissistic act, with a rather miserable Pope looking on; a satire, perhaps. Napoleon's mother Maria Letizia Ramolino is positioned under the arch in a place that renders her superior to the Pope. Consequently we see a tension arise between traditional procedures of monarchy (as seen through its dynamic with religion) and the emerging dominance of the military sphere. Napoleon seems simultaneously to seek conventional legitimacy, but with a greater emphasis on temporal power.

Napoleon wears a laurel wreath, which he is said to have been wearing as he arrived and kept on during the ceremony. His attire aligns with this Roman imperial sentiment. Furthermore, the crown is termed "Crown of Charlemagne", which recalls the King of the Franks and the emperor of the Romans in the 8th and 9th centuries CE. This differs from the previous monarch, King Louis XVI. The succession of Roman Emperors, although dynastic in the early stages, became increasingly militaristic, particularly midway through the 3rd century CE (250–280). Napoleon's success, his very identity, lay in the military sphere.

Practice Summary

It has often been implicitly, or explicitly, assumed that external candidates are better suited for radical change. There is mixed research and practical support for this. Alongside forming a mandate, the board has to have a strategy position regarding the choice of internal and external candidates. The board needs initially to formulate what the organization needs to be, and be clear about understanding the challenges it is facing and what its leadership should be. Leaving this to the new CEO, seeking an outsider so as to safeguard oneself, is risky as the right leader from the inside, with capacity to lead despite turmoil, may have the cultural capital to bring forward deeper cultural and identity changes. An initial mandate needs to be established, before specific criteria are identified with regards to the leadership skills necessary. The formulation of a mandate in a succession situation necessitates shifting between a focus on the past and the future.

Focussing on the past will include an analysis of former leadership tenure: achievements, shortfalls, strengths and weaknesses of the leader and the capability of the organization.

Focussing on the future will include an analysis of strengths, weaknesses, opportunities and threats. The type of leadership necessary.

Mandates including deep cultural change that also affect social identities are challenging for any new leader. A board, or a new CEO, should not ignore a process of exploring the question of "What we are not?", and whether this shadow can be included into the existing organizational identity, or rather represents an opportunity for a new venture. In certain instances, incubation can replace a succession process altogether.

References

Chatterjee, S., & White, L. (2019, August 4). HSBC axes CEO Flint in shock shift to speed up strategy, *Reuters*.

Giambatista, R. C., Rowe, W. G., & Riaz, S. (2005). Nothing succeeds like succession: A critical review of leader succession literature since 1994, *The Leadership Quarterly*, 16(6), 963–991.

Ismail, S., Malone, M., & van Geest, Y. (2014). *Exponential organizations*. Diversion Books.

8

THE HANDOVER AND CEO ENTRY

An effective handover to a new CEO is often conflated with the whole succession process or can be seen as a mere detail. It is often also discussed from the individual leader's trajectory and for how to exit and enter in the best way. I have in Chapters 3 and 4 covered some of the emotional issues that a leader has to look out for when exiting a role. In particular a process of loss and mourning as the road turns toward new roles and activities is important. Also the board, on behalf of the organization and their reactions, needs to be aware of the wide range of emotions and group dynamics that a succession can trigger. A handover process is the last step of the succession strategy and will be influenced by how well the other strategies have been executed. The same can be said about the new leader's immersion, or entry, into the organization. Trust in the process is a invaluable platform for a new top leader.

What I will show in this chapter is that the handover is the beginning of the leader-follower process. Followership implies the establishing of trust and processes of personal authority. The latter contrasts with the more destructive political processes that can occur, with hidden agendas, around a new leader. At the handover the executive control is transferred. It requires the involvement of the governing body, incumbent and successor alike. In academic research, the concept of a favourable transaction atmosphere has been proposed, while family business literature has referred to the importance of knowledge transfer in succession (Boyd et al., 2015). I use the term favourable transition atmosphere as capturing the work needed to create a good handover. In a well-handled succession process, and even in some where there were faults, the outgoing executive is ready to move on and the incomer is well prepared and eager to take the reins.

The legacy of a successful previous leader can weigh heavily on a new CEO. If one is recruited from the outside one might be pitched against a much-loved leader. If one is recruited from inside one might feel the legacy more as a burden. Against that, an insider new CEO might find it easier to create a dialogue that is respectful to a much-loved leader and at the same time trigger necessary change. Any new leader could feel that there is a continual judgement, being seen as a relative failure owing to unrealistic expectations. This is a problem for the organization, as well as for the leader. Well-managed handovers can mitigate many such emotional issues. I will in this chapter describe the hostile welcome of a CEO I worked closely with and how she overcame fierce internal opposition. I also describe how sequencing of different transitions connected to the handover with the CEO role is important, a process of a delicate dance with employees, and how the incumbent–successor relations can play out. In addition to being used for finding candidates a headhunter might be active in the preparation and process of handover (Gilmore, 2007). In Box 8.1 the opposite of a delicate dance or favourable transition atmosphere is shown. It also illustrates what has been discussed before: a leadership logic is upheld in the succession system of any organization and, while it selects a leader aligning with the leadership logic, it also gives the leadership a symbolic value.

BOX 8.1 COMBAT TO DEATH: REX NEMORENSIS

In Roman times, Rex Nemorensis was the title of the priest and head of the Diana Temple (Pascal, 1976). Diana was a goddess for Rome's neighborhood Aventine, where plebeians and slaves lived, as oppose to patricians. The rules for succession were unusual. The post of Rex Nemorensis was reserved for a former slave who had escaped from his owner. If any fugitive slave managed to enter the temple, this would be considered a challenge to the sitting Rex Nemorensis. A battle to the death would determine who would have the position. Succession where the successor has to be killed for a hand-over to happen can reflect a overly self absorbed new leader or reflect other significant leadership logics and political contexts. Some of the same brutal succession, with symbolic killings, can be seen in organizations today and actual killing often occurs within criminal organizations.

Source: Alamy

Most often priesthoods in Rome, recruited from patricians, had an elective system of succession. The Rex Nemorensis (the king of the wood) and Rex Sacrorum (King of the sacred) were titled as King yet those eligible for the respective titles were polar opposites in social position. The former was an ex-slave and the latter would have to be a patrician. Using 'Rex' in the title was a reference to the older Roman tradition of kingship before 509 BC, when the killing of the last king led to the establishment of the republic of Rome. Some privileges and duties of the king were transferred to priests' titles and function. The post of Rex Sacrorum was the most prestigious. The role of priests in Rome was to attend to the society's relationship with the gods. They were given roles that addressed important Roman concepts: *pax, fortuna,* and *salus.* Each role and leadership logic, in one way or another, ensure that the governance and administration of Rome and its empire was aligned with divine will. The priesthood was banned from political or military involvement, so that their religious role would not be misused. Rex Sacrorum and Rex Nemorensis can be seen as mirror images; two Kings, one belonging to the top and the other to the bottom of Roman religion's hierarchy.

On the surface it might appear that Rex Nemorensis offered, in symbolic form, some hope of social mobility for slaves provided they have managed to escape. The Romans, including the slaves, were deeply religious and superstitious. We must bear in mind that a slave revolt was a very real and deep-seated fear among the ruling class of Rome as the patricians where greatly outnumbered by slaves. Spartacus, a Thracian soldier, raised a slave revolt which turned into a full-scale war that Crassus eventually quelled in 71 BCE. The threat slaves represented might account for the brutal succession system as it encapsulated hope and destructive in the hand-over.

8.1 Hostile CEO Welcome

One research case by the author involved an in-depth study of a museum and university. The research method was action learning, sometimes called collaborative research (Osnes, 2016, 2020). Initially it was a focus on helping the CEO into the role, which was predicted to be a difficult process. The research project developed into a ten year research project where the board function and processes of chair and CEO succession take place over time and affect the organization and its leadership. The research followed several chair and CEO succession processes; a total of three chair and two CEO transitions. After an initial six-year tenure, at the end of her contract, the CEO agreed on a new three-year contract. Two years before her exit a successor for the chair, started.

The start of the project, began with the entry of a newly appointed CEO and the implementation of a new type of board. Previously, a top leader at a college or institute would be elected by the academics within the unit for a term of four years. With a new succession system for appointing a CEO, a new and broader succession pool, comprising not only internal academics, came into effect. Furthermore, an academic board structure where the elected head would be both chair of the board and administrative leader was replaced by a separate chair and CEO.

This was a radical shift from the established succession system and logic on leadership within the university sector at the time, the late 1990s to early 2000s. The Ministry of Education, acting on behalf of the public, and the university would act as "owners" of the museum. Prior to 1999, a university law regulated the governing structure. The latter was of significance as the leaders initiating the change in the governance structure had to negotiate with the Ministry of Education so as to be allowed to experiment with the governing structure, to enable a radically different type of leadership for an organization in deep crisis. The notion of deep crisis was a general conclusion within the university and museum, but despite this consensus there was a deep ambivalence about changing the governance structure, and with it, the leadership logic and social identity provided by the organization. The quote below came from one of the presidents of the university reflecting on the turmoil triggered by these changes.

> It is something that happens in science; also in art and cultural life, where some products, tasks and tools become like a part of your family. It is as if it is your identity! So you think that you cannot live without it. When we get these transitions, we feel them as a combination of personal loss, loss of a personal domain, loss of an existential legitimacy in some sense. After all, this is why we are here, this is our core task!

The mandate for the first new CEO and Chair was to improve research output, resolve internal conflicts that had been festering for years and to create a more innovative and publicly visible museum. It was also part of the mandate to implement a radically new type of leadership, which was connected to a radical redesign of the board. Initially the CEO was met with a hostile welcome. Revolt followed as the "experiment" was seen as replacing a democratic leadership system. A significant group of academics placed themselves in direct opposition to the changes in the governance structure and new leader, adopting a "fight by any means" reaction, as if they were in survival mode. The academic unions went on strike and for a whole year there was no formal leadership structure. The following quote, from a union representative, an elected member of the board, reflects both the process and achievement of the exiting CEO, years later.

> I'm now a great admirer of the CEO ... It does not mean that I'm blind to her weaknesses and all that ... but I must say – I wouldn't have survived what she had to deal with, never ... I would have been destroyed ... what she had to tolerate! The personal attacks internally, all this criticism in public, in the news, in private, a lockdown with the union. And she just said "pffht!" to all that ... she just marched on! Unaffected ... and with a huff! ... I think she is fabulous.

The old succession system had led to what in any other type of organization would have been seen as a collapse. Implicit in the elective system was a marginalization of leadership, so research would not be influenced by political appointees. Such marginalization of leadership – the polar opposite of idealization of the heroic, charismatic leader – reflects just another type of wishful thinking. Typically, the academic in post had neither the preparation nor the motivation for the role, and was a reluctant leader. If a leader during his or her tenure had implemented controversial decisions, this could be uncomfortable, especially since they would be due to return to the academic community. Other threats, such as colleagues' retribution as they would sit in committees determining research applications, was also feared. The succession system therefore made sure that the elected leaders rarely would take any controversial decision, address conflicts among employees and leaders, address harassment or develop strategies that could affect some fields negatively. Another unfortunate aspect of the rotating leadership system was that the elected leader was chair of the board and head of unit, and the board would often micromanage the execution of the few strategies that it was possible to develop.

The pool of suitable candidates to succeed the first CEO was limited. The specifications were demanding and precise for the next CEO: they would be expected to have professor competence within one of the academic fields within the museum and also have top leadership experience. A unique pool did become available, of geologists with professor roles or competence from within the energy business, producing candidates with top leadership experience from corporate businesses. There had never been, at the museum or university, any systematic training of academics in leadership and management and no internal candidates for the role. Leadership roles were generally seen as a chore that would disrupt the academic career, and academics would end up informally taking turns, choosing to have a leadership role depending on when it would suit their research interests and do the least harm.

The fierce resistance that the change initially provoked from inside the institution was more than mere opposition to the logic of the governance system. It was a more visceral and cultural reaction, fearing a loss of identity, loss of role and possibly even loss of expertise. Several fantasies were spread, creating fears about the entry of the new CEO which included that commercial interests would crowd out interest in research quality, that a directive leadership style could become too hierarchical and the strengths of the democratic tradition would be undermined. Ultimately, the CEO achieved a balance, being able to demonstrate that a stronger financial basis could help, rather than hinder, research quality, and she encouraged distributed leadership within the institution. This was not clear to everyone at the outset, as the quote below illustrates:

> There has been a fear that ... someone would come from the outside and turn things upside down, not detail-wise but more generally. And I work at an institute where there has been a comfort with a manager type of top leader as it was in many ways better for what one had in mind intellectually. I was not really a leader because a manager takes care of things, and is led by a collegial body that make more or less sensible decisions. The last 5 to 10 years major players have started to say that it is a question about leadership, in a different way from just solving on-going problems and ensuring that tasks are being safeguarded. It is actually to think how the unit can develop in the long term, and how we work to get the most out of those resources we have, both human and economic. And now it is coming.

Some aspects of the succession wheel were overlooked initially. The board was new and had itself to change old habits. Micro-management of a top leader was the norm. With a separation of the roles of chair and top leader there were more checks and balances, and more executive authority could be given to the CEO. One reflection on this struggle, as I encounter such change of a board's habits in other work, is how difficult it is for even seasoned and highly resourceful top leaders to change a system that relates to power and authority. In the case of the museum, where the board was fully supporting the redesign of the board and they took part in the process, it was still an emotional hurdle when one was relating to the new top leader in a new way. This took two years to be finalized, along with the reforms to the board. Failure to address this successfully could have led to the resignation of the CEO. In the event, the CEO negotiated with the board and eventually secured the authority for many of the strategic decisions necessary, and the board developed a system for keeping her accountable.

Despite all the challenges, the CEO managed to overcome her hostile welcome. At the start of her tenure many ad-hoc structures had to be created so as to ensure strategy processes, such as research grant applications. This created a positive experience with cross-academic collaboration, initially highly resisted, and success – somewhat to the academics' surprise – in securing major funding for some research projects. This enhanced the credibility of the CEO. It improved the process of wider understanding of the challenges and the rationale for strategic work and leadership. The strike ended and a normal leadership structure, after one year, was in place.

8.2 Sequencing Transitions

One important revelation in the museum research was how important it is to make sure that a succession is sequenced well with other successions and transitions in and around the board. When the board structure was changed all the members, the chair and the CEO, started what were fixed-year tenures in the same year. This threatened to create an unfortunate sequencing ten years later, with all key individuals departing at the same time. After the first CEO had been in the role for nine years, the organization prepared the succession for a new CEO. Many of the top researchers and staff were the same, but the organization had been through a long process of change and consolidation. Suddenly one was aware that the chair, board members and the CEO would all leave within a period of one year. Crucially the chair would leave first leaving a new chair, and new board members, to recruit a new CEO. This created the risk that the board would lack historical perspective and familiarity with the strategic discussion, and would be inadequately prepared for recruiting a new leader.

The sequence of appointment of board members and the new chair had to align so that the CEO left first. One new external board member was chosen with the intention of taking over as chair after the succession of the CEO was complete. In addition only half of the academic board members were replaced. Careful thinking about the sequence of tenures made it possible to ensure that there was a solid group of board members, combining deep knowledge of the strategic issues with new ideas and perspectives. If there is not a time limited contract with the CEO, the best practice is to have a constant shift of new and old members so one has a balance of continuity and institutional knowledge with new members and fresh perspectives. Such a mix can increase tension in the board, but this can spur robust debate and discovery of innovative ideas.

Orchestrating the handovers requires careful thinking about the sequence of tenures: how long the contract of the chair lasts, the contract with board members and a possible contract limited by time for the CEO. In itself this consideration is an argument for having fixed tenures for roles of chair and CEO. In the UK, for example, official guidance is that a chair, or any board member, is not to be in post for more than nine years. The implication is that a board member, if planning or designated to become chair of the board, the period one has as board member will limit the time one will be chair of the board. A fixed term on behalf of the CEO, even though it might be resisted by candidates, has the advantage that it automatically triggers the board to be more active in succession planning during a leadership tenure.

In the case of the museum, ten years after an ultimately very successful CEO was met with internal hostility, a new CEO received a completely different welcome. The whole organization, including all the academics, felt the former CEO had been a big success. A new governance structure had, through her success and that of two chairs of the board, been consolidated and was generally trusted. Similar changes in governance structures had been implemented across the university. At this point the university had also started training academics for leadership roles, creating a new generation with more modern views on leadership. Despite this the new CEO was a professor with top leadership experience from outside the university. He would retire after a tenure of six years and a mandate of consolidation of major changes inside the organization, building on a former tenure of entrepreneurship and innovation, was developed.

8.3 Delicate Dance and Followership

The 90-day rule, referring to the first three months of a new CEO's tenure, has been popularized since a leadership book of that name became influential, but there's little hard evidence that this particular length of time has special significance. The research base does indicate that the first weeks of a tenure are important; also, however, that being too active, and making too many major decisions, can be a mistake, especially for an external candidate (Torres & Tolman, 2012). In some sectors, the pace of change is high, and organizations require constant change and adaptation. Striking the right balance between analysis and action is always a challenge. To create a committed team from the leaders and employees an external CEO "crashing into" the organization is not a good way to establish trust. Only a crisis that needs to be solved immediately, issues such as widespread incompetence or fraud, would justify that a new CEO makes radical changes on arrival. One can use the first 90 days to make changes and sift out leaders who will not be staying in a leadership role. Radical measures should not become a piece of theatre for a stock market or other shareholders or a board. If such bold action fails, or is unnecessary, it achieves the opposite of what was intended; the leader looks weak rather than strong. It can also create a fearful and politicized work environment with key employees leaving.

A better guide than the concept of imposing oneself in 90 days is that of the delicate dance. This metaphor is a term coined by researcher Handler (1990) where a new CEO is in a dance where she/he has to establish a relationship with the board, other top leaders and become a member, and leader, of the organization. This is a difficult balance as a sense of being rejected can occur. At the same time the CEO should not lose the freedom of action that might be necessary. It is important to understand the culture and the way in which decisions are taken, and services and products created.

In the museum case, as immersion processes go, the second CEO appointment involved a smooth handover. A delicate dance in the immersion involves signals that are given and interpreted, certain processes and needs for knowledge that are informally and formally discussed. It is either explicit, or implicitly guessed at, what the new leader wants to know about. The process can be done with speed if necessary. It allows for the organization to be seen as a reservoir of knowledge where relevance of knowledge and experience is negotiated in the entry process. When the process is understood as being an institutional dynamic, employees, advisors and leaders can see themselves as a reservoir of knowledge and information available for the new leader.

Disruptive welcomes, more subtle than the open revolt described in the museum case, can involve the use or withholding of knowledge and information, frustrating the new leader. Such obstructive dynamics can reflect disappointment over the lack of an internal candidate being selected, or a strong sense of loyalty to the former leader. It can also be a result of the new CEO "crashing into" the organization. Lack of a delicate dance can lead to the new leader being overwhelmed, so he/she gets bogged down. This might be done as part of a process of putting forward one's own agenda, or the agenda of one department. Such dynamics reflect a highly politicized organization.

8.4 Incumbent–Successor Dynamics

Effective handover can be disrupted by a failure of letting go and stepping up on behalf of the incumbent and successor. I make a differentiation between the group and organization as being in a succession process while the exiting and entering leader is in a leadership transition. They will have their own role and career trajectories and the hand over is a junction where these transitions meet. The board can represent a buffer zone for the personal dynamics that can be triggered in the preparation for, duration or aftermath of this junction. Some dialogues between the incumbent and successor are often necessary. It can be helpful – in the case of a lame duck period – to consult the incoming leader about decisions that cannot be postponed, and that could have a major impact on the next tenure. Sometimes there are personnel issues within the organization that only the CEO should be privy to and thereby need to be handed over to a new leader in a direct dialogue. In the case of an internally recruited leader, the immersion process is different. Obviously, less time is needed to get to know the organization. The board has to take care that the relationship between the incumbent and successor is not too close. The new CEO has to be allowed to operate with a certain freedom, and not too much loyalty to the former leader. It is possible that in these cases the relationship can sour; rivalry and envy are features of big egos.

The relationship between an incumbent and successor is more delicate, and complicated, within family ownership and family businesses. When an influential leader has stepped down from a senior role, such as chair or CEO, often he or she is still an owner, and retains significant interest. This can create actual or perceived clashes of power, but this is not inevitable. Some move successfully to a role of mentor. This was the case in an Israeli tourism company, one of the cases studied in a cross-cultural research project. A married couple had founded it. The wife oversaw the accounts at the firm and remained an asset to the company without interfering in the management structure. Tellingly, the quote illustrates some of the complexity of the handover in an owner-family. Noteworthy in this exchange is the informality and affection, and use of humour when reflecting the acceptance of what could have been torn by friction and tensions:

> My mother is still head of accounts [90 years old], and she still finds these mistakes. It's a mystery to me how she still does it. She then wants to explain to you what the mistakes that you made were. She gets someone to come and fetch you. This happens to everyone, employees and family members. If someone in the family is told to get me I know what the message is before it is said. It's a glow in how they move and their voice, "Tata wants to see you!" I'm now 70 years old [President and active owner]. I do not want to be in such an operational role any more. My brother and I have discussed this, and I took two of our children aside and talked to them. We want them to take over some leadership duties. They asked me, in a funny way, "What about Tata?" I told them, "Do not draw the wrong conclusion, I will not retire, I want a role where I can do more of the things I like, developing other things. I will also sit and find the mistakes that you make.
>
> (President, Second generation owner, Israel)

Humour is rarely discussed in management textbooks, but can be helpful in terms of reducing tension and maintaining relationships. It is more likely to be a factor in family firms, but not exclusively so. A joke can be more specific and possibly a veiled criticism in the same way as self-deprecation is an indirect way of self-critique; unless one uses it to invite people to contradict the deprecation and by this get some support. Above, in the quote, the humour is used to convey how the family is bound by affection and respect, in so doing managing any feelings of frustration and possibly affront.

8.5 Organizational Identity Shadows

Carl Gustav Jung, one of the founders of psychotherapy, explored the notion of our identity shadows. Throughout life we form our identities through activities and roles. At any stage options may have to be left unexplored or not developed. Such identity shadows are not always conscious and can be a possible dark side of an individual. Identity shadows, when they become conscious, can be hidden strength and a source for new types of identities developed through new solutions or roles. Bringing into consciousness means expanding what one identifies as and might be what in more popular leadership guidance is called being outside one's comfort zone. One can explore, and include, previously overlooked possibilities for how one identifies oneself. It can be usefully applied at an organizational level. In a way shadows are unavoidable. As a person or organization one makes choices that exclude other attractive possibilities and over time these can determine strategic direction and the development of a culture.

A CEO's entry might explicitly or implicitly have a mandate of cultural and social identity change. The entering CEO will easily come to personify the change of social identity, and often this provokes a strong pushback. Change that triggers strong emotions, when not managed, can mean that the strategy argument is ignored. If a desired change is transformational, this implies changes in organizational identity that often affect employees' and other leaders' identities. This often triggers resistance and anger. If some employees or other stakeholders feel that the change threatens the essence of the organization – its culture, their identity – it can lead to a brain-drain and can also undermine performance.

A board needs to understand the limits of cultural change and, beyond a certain point, changes of deeply held values and identities; a company cannot be reinvented. One of the most radical types of transformation, that some business leaders aspire to, is to change from a stable corporate way of working to a more nimble, entrepreneurial firm. Within strategy thinking this is often a response to a disruptive competitor that may be using new technology or a radically different business model. The difference between an established corporation and an innovative start-up is the difference between a ruthlessly efficient operation where operational cost is minimized, to a more experimental way of working where the cost of a failure is tolerated if it is genuinely innovative with rich learning opportunities. In practice, larger firms have found it difficult to make this transition within the existing corporate structure, and a change in leader is not enough. The change required in culture, leadership mandate and ways of working might stretch the corporation beyond the point of elasticity. Beyond a certain point, transformation is not possible, and a new venture has to be founded. This helps explain why there are limits to cultural change, and sometimes a new organization has to be formed as an alternative. Boards need to keep this in mind, as do new CEOs.

A succession is one way of transforming a company but another alternative, discussed more in Chapter 10, titled "Succession or Incubation?" shows how family owners incubate new ventures, rather than use a succession which could disrupt an efficient, but not overly innovative, organization. Referring to a corporate setting Salim Ismail, former head of the incubator at Yahoo and co-author of *Exponential Organizations*, claims new innovative firms "are ten times better, faster and cheaper than yours" – referring to their ability to use big data and algorithms to scale upwards rapidly, without necessarily growing large in terms of number of employees (Ismail et al., 2014). Even if this comes across as exaggeration, there is no doubting the inherent problem of creating radically new services and products from within an established firm: the investment and management time required would take so much away from the existing revenue stream that managers will always rein in the new venture to protect the existing. I will discuss this more in depth in Chapter 9, where I describe succession and incubation as two alternative or parallel strategies that maintain parts of the organization to be developed in an evolutionary way and rather use incubation to generate more innovation.

Practice Summary

Successions have faltered because of problems at the handover stage despite a good match with the mandate and other aspects that were well thought through. Should the worst happen, the costs to the organization and individuals concerned can be severe. The handover is in this way a reflection of how well the mandate has been constructed, as well as the definition of the leadership wish list and creation of the succession pool. The issue of executive discretion (Chapter 11), the deal with the leader, which reflects issues of status, leadership drive and power and authority, is important. These themes are covered in Chapters 10 and 11. Chapter 11 explores incubation strategy as a succession process.

References

Boyd, B., Royer, S., Pei, R., & Zhang, X. (2015). Knowledge transfer in family business successions: Implications of knowledge types and transaction atmospheres. *Journal of Family Business Management, 5*(1), 17–37.

Gilmore, T. (2007). Headhunting: Psychodynamics of potential spaces created in the executive search process. *Socio-analysis, 9*, 63.

Handler, W. C. (1990). Succession in family firms: A mutual role adjustment between entrepreneur and next-generation family members. *Entrepreneurship Theory and Practice, 15*(1), 37–52.

Ismail, S. (2014). *Exponential organizations: Why new organizations are ten times better, faster, and cheaper than yours (and what to do about it).* Diversion Books.

Osnes, G. (2016). Strategizing Successions: Sibling Loyalty in a French Case. In G. Osnes (Ed.), *Family Capitalism* (pp. 56–67). Routledge.

Osnes, G (2020). Part I; A historical analysis of "our leader": A university ten-year study on executive succession and affect. *Organisational and Social Dynamics, 20*(2), 1–20.

Pascal, C. Bennett (1976). "Rex Nemorensis." *Numen, 23*(1), 23–39. *JSTOR*, www.jstor.org/stable/3269555. p. 35.

Torres, R., & Tollman P. (2012). Five myths of a CEO's first 100 days, *Harvard Business Review*, https://hbr.org/2012/01/five-myths-of-a-ceos-first-100

9

SUCCESSION OR INCUBATION?

Successions are often limited to the transfer of a single top executive role. Regardless of how a succession is triggered it is a strategic opportunity to bring renewal. Yet other options are possible that could lead to renewal. In this chapter I will address how the need for renewal through innovation should not be conflated with an executive succession. Rather than changing a top leader, or possibly together with a top leader succession process, one can incubate something new. As such incubation could be the renewal strategy that will influence if there will be a succession process. Readers should note that much theory on incubation has been developed so as to help organizations to be innovative and entrepreneurial.

Here I will show that a board, or top executive team or owner, can externalize the process of incubating new ventures so as to protect the efficient and more traditional management of the main company. It is an inherent disruptive and complex process to develop new ventures. It is not to disregard strategies making an established company more innovative. I will show how one should consider, if one needs to have more innovation, an incubation process in addition to or instead of a succession. It might be the current leader is steadily leading the main business through growth but would not be a good leader for the long term, when there often would be a need to develop new ventures of products or processes. A succession could disrupt the growth and efficient machinery of the main business.

Incubation can be used as an identity project, addressing the "What we don't do", or "What we are not set up to do". It can be exemplified by how Nestlé set up a separate company, Nespresso, in 1986. It was founded to explore the potential for higher quality espresso-style coffee in individual pods. The inventor was a rocket scientist, Eric Favre, a Swiss national who decided to prove his Italian wife wrong when she commented that the Swiss could not make the best coffee. He joined Nestlé's packaging department in 1975, at a time when it was famous for instant coffee. He made his invention after studying the principles of how espresso machines worked by aerating the hot water as it passed through the ground coffee. Initially, there was resistance within Nestlé. With the establishment of a separate company the invention moved from a prototype to a highly successful new venture. There were initial difficulties prompting Favre to leave in 1991 (Simon, 2016). The Nespresso machines became hugely popular in the years after 2000. The lesson is, for the board, the incubation of a new venture might be an alternative to an otherwise unnecessary succession process or, for a new CEO, rather than challenging an otherwise good and efficient culture, incubation of ventures might be less disruptive and taxing on one's leadership.

9.1 Ownership Evolution

The incubation capability, rather than or in parallel with succession process, is best illustrated drawing on cases from family ownership and leadership roles. I have elsewhere (e.g. Osnes, 2016) explored strategies for family ownership, intergenerational transmission and family dynamics in depth. It build on what clients and research cases cases would be able to develop of agility and complexity in their strategy processes. As much research on family ownership has focused on the family business, certain intriguing strategies that owner families are doing has been less explored. It has perpetuated a part myth that family owners often fail in the third generation. What is often not shown is how a family might have leveraged a business, the knowledge or social capital they have, and started other ventures while selling the business they are the most identified with. Choosing to incubate a new venture can be combined or done in parallel with a succession.

Elsewhere there are plenty of examples of how successions in family ownership and businesses fail (e.g. Gersik, 1997). Departing from this limited framing I will show families might evolve the ownership in a way that it, from the outside, would appear to be a failed ownership and succession process. In family ownership a top leadership role is often assumed to be held by one person, or a couple, when the business was founded. During the course of generational transitions several other combinations are possible. What I call monolithic succession processes, leaders exiting and entering into a singular role, is no longer an assumption that always holds in family firm successions. With increasing agility, the family unit are using their ownership to incubate new companies and new roles rather than focusing on one company and one top leadership role.

Strategy theory addressing non-family organizations such as corporations has developed an increasing focus on how to generate corporate intrapreneurship and innovative solutions with regards to new businesses, business models, products or work processes. I will show how family ownership can tolerate a high level tension leading to innovation or creative tension. It is based on having strong emotional bonds, cooperation across traditional gender and age stereotypes, distribution of leadership, development of new types of roles and focus on purpose. Rather than the main, still profit-making, business taking on such a challenge, the creation of a new venture and leadership role reduces the pressure of change in the top leadership role.

Throughout the cases here, drawn from different parts of the world, western notions of seniors retiring at a specific time, the next generation getting experience from outside of the business and choosing only one member of the family to work in the business are challenged. In addition, social changes, difference in social safety nets, reoccurring economic recessions and political challenges, such as adapting to the reduction of global warming, influence succession and the birth of new ventures. What were earlier seen as best practices within family ownership and leadership of their businesses are a highly complex domain and should now be up for review.

Social Change and Ownership

Another research finding relevant for succession and incubation in family ownership is the role of women. Far more women have a higher education compared with earlier generations, in all regions of the world, and this is changing leadership succession for family owners. Often women have had invisible leadership, or ownership, that has been significant for the business. It is often assumed this is emotional support and in that way researchers, often male, had chosen to explore what is congruent with cultural biases on gender. In an earlier study, and consistently through seven best practice cases, we found that women often had financial control, did the accounts or at the minimum had a veto power on financial investment. In Chapter 2 I described a northern European family owner with a tradition of women in strong informal roles. Interviews in family ownership cases we did uncovered that a leading role for women was nothing new in the business: the wife of the founder generation in Israel had been heavily involved in setting up and running the original business. In a northern European case a founder couple had set up a mineral water business, the wife was an exceptionally resourceful individual, having taken up a philanthropic role in the community and caring for a sibling group of orphaned adolescents, but had also been responsible for financial accounts and later for manufacturing in the business.

The northern European family, in the third to forth generation succession process, developed a distributed leadership system (Haug, 2016). The female third generation owner got her rightful place on the board that represented the invisible role she had held for years. Her daughter and a male cousin were seen as future leaders in the business. Rather than focusing on one top leadership role, a board with a non-family chair developed complementary leadership roles, which were successfully held for 15 years. Such distribution of leadership (Gronn, 2017) has most likely been undocumented but in use historically.

In a study of what is often seen as the highly patriarchal Wallenberg family, the researcher Lindgren (2002) showed such distributed leadership and control. The Wallenbergs control a significant number of listed companies in Sweden and have been influential entrepreneurs and owners continuously for two centuries, not confining themselves to one company. Over several generations power has been distributed between two brothers or two cousins in addition to having a powerful CEO and non-family leaders. The family's approach has always involved a combination of distributed leadership and entrepreneurial alternatives to conventional, individualistic succession limited to one company/one senior role. The lessons from the two cases are that one should not make the mistake of thinking a family ownership succession is about centralized control. Many families owners, as in the Wallenberg family, have been seen as having centralized control when in reality there has been a distribution of control and roles.

Family Owners Evolving

I found a similar distributed leadership system in place in what one might otherwise assume would be a context that was hostile to female leadership. It is a research case from before Israel was a state and a tourism business, founded by a Lutheran Arab couple in the 1920s in Palestine, at the time governed by the British, before the establishment of Israel in 1948. In modern Israel, the family has managed to maintain a non-sectarian hiring policy, with both Jewish and Muslim staff. They were strict in maintaining their non-discriminatory policies, and employees who did not respect this were asked to leave. Family's loyalty, therefore, was first and foremost to their values, rather than any particular institution. Such value based purpose is a feature of many long-lasting business-owning families. This family managed to maintain this policy through challenging periods of the Israeli-Palestine conflict, not merely surviving but building a mini-cluster of successful tourism-related businesses.

The firm was a touring and hotel business with customers, mostly religious groups from Europe and the USA, and they would design and arrange the visit to Israel or elsewhere in the region. A first succession, in the mid-20th century, involved imaginative alternatives to the traditional or monolithic archetype. Two sons, both of whom had studied in the USA, returned to Israel to become involved in the family firm. The mother, the female founder and 90 years old at the time of the research, had always had an informal ownership role with her husband in addition to assorted leadership roles within the business. At the time I researched the case she had an exit role as head of accounts. In their first succession, instead of a single competition for the one role, the family divided the enterprise into three companies; the original tour company, a bus and a hotel company. One of the sons, the more risk-averse, managed the original tour business, while the other secured financing to set up a hotel. The mother handed the business over to two brothers with complementary skills, different approaches to business and different levels of appetite for risk.

To the outside world, and to customers, the firm operated as one brand, but internally the lines of responsibility and exposure to risk were distinct. By the third generation, the business had expanded internationally and encompassed tours, a travel agency and a small chain of hotels. A non-family Managing Director (MD) was employed. The new entrepreneurial options resolved a potential dilemma over succession, while increasing opportunities and revenue for the family. In the planning of the transition to the third generation, with several daughters involved in the business, the family maintained a high degree of flexibility in combining work and family roles, allowing periods where a family member was not involved in one of the businesses. The emphases lay on strong relationships and matching roles to individual needs. One might look at the ecosystem of this business and the futures of the third generation. With an Arabic background they have limited attractive career possibilities.

9.2 Monolithic and Distributed Leadership

Family as an ownership group has some unique options, and challenges, with regards to the succession strategy for top leadership roles. The family can leverage on existing assets and expertise when entrepreneurial alternatives are being created as succession strategies. Developing such imaginative entrepreneurial alternatives is not a new development, but is often lost in succession studies. A succession study often confines itself to the established company, not spin offs or how the family may have an overall strategy for a cluster of firms. For some time, enterprising families have created clusters of businesses (Michael-Tsabari et al., 2014), which in some cases extend to start-up firms set up not by family members themselves, but former employees and others within the region.

The incubation option, and the choice of a less centralized leadership system within a monolithic succession, challenges old myths around family ownership succession. The most familiar narrative is that of a sole, male entrepreneur, and the anticipation of crisis once the founder retires and the consequent problems inherent in nepotism, limiting the talent pool. Over the last 20 years, after the researcher Gersick (1997) popularized the practice of ownership forums so as to contain these dynamics, many successful families have started using these types of social structures to contain family dynamics and guide orderly successions. They are designed primarily for family firms, but could be used by other owners. Family-owned firms are increasingly appointing non-family senior executives, while family members retain strategic leadership roles.

I explore other best practices that family owners, and their leaders and advisors, can use. In the handover to the next generation, the family can hand over leadership roles and the ownership role relating to an already existing business. They can hand over in a monolithic way where there is one company and one top leadership role. They can also do a succession in a more distributed way; there may be several leadership roles in one or several companies that they own. Incubation is an entrepreneurial alternative that can include serial entrepreneurship and cluster ownership (Michael-Tsabari, 2014). The examples highlighting the importance of strategic choice, and shifting between them, are shown in Figure 9.1.

As shown in the Israel case and the following Chinese case, there are many ways a family can balance the distribution of leadership in succession or between succession and incubation processes. One research case for this book, prepared by a Chinese colleague Olive Yanli Hou, will be used to show how both incubation and succession options were used by a business-owning family. I will show how a family's values and emotional ties are a key a part of the leadership logic in family ownership. Lastly I describe how family offices, often used by later generations in high net-worth families, can be used as a succession and incubation vehicle.

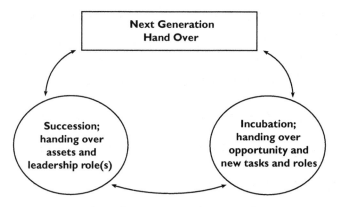

Figure 9.1 Succession and Incubation in Family Ownership

9.3 FOTILE: Family Incubation in China

The FOTILE business illustrates an understudied phenomena; how cluster ownership in families are a part of the development or co-exist in cluster regions. Such clusters can be seen in northern Italy in what is a cluster for the fashion industry and in Oslo and the marine shipping industry. I have shown before how a family did this for making wooden toys in China (Osnes, 2016). The following is the case of an enterprising Chinese family who had overseen the creation of a cluster of firms in the electrical goods sector, including the successful FOTILE brand of kitchen goods. There was a sole male founder of the original firm, Lixiang Mao, who had originally begun a company making TV parts in 1985. Researcher Olive Yanli Hou interviewed Lixiang and studied the case as part of the research for this book.

FOTILE is based in Cixi (慈溪), a noted cluster for electrical appliance manufacturing in China. The current company was not the first, but is currently one of the major companies in the locality. Cluster regions possess many advantages for businesses, including manufacturing. They offer local knowledge, a skilled, specialist workforce and owners with a strong social network and access to capital. Also, they mean that global companies know where to go for certain goods or services. Another Chinese family in our research, initially a producer of wooden toys, but later owning several gaming, retail and tech firms, helped nurture a cluster of related firms in its region.

Co-entrepreneurs, Distributed Leadership and Incubation

In the very early period of Lixiang's first firm, it was successful and as his workload grew, he appointed his wife, whose abilities in management and accounting came from a previous role as production manager at a knitting factory. She became deputy director. Unfortunately, owing to overproduction and changes in government policy, the TV parts business hit crisis. Lixiang Mao set up a new firm producing electronic igniters and lighters. This thrived for several years but again the firm faced crisis, following strong competition and price pressures in the early to mid-1990s. At this point, the founder invited his son, Zhongqun Mao, to help him restore growth. In the meantime, his daughter Jisheng had become involved, running a spin-off firm, a barbecue business, with her husband. The father and daughter started it together, but it became the daughter's business. At the time of writing she was still managing the business as a separate company – she is also on the family council for her brother's business, and has some shares in that company. From this point a cluster began to form.

Social Context and Second Generation Motivation

The involvement of the son ultimately led to dramatic diversification and business success, but this was not inevitable or obvious at the time. Zhongqun, the founder's son, was academically gifted, with many career options. In 1994 he was pursuing his PhD in the USA, having earned a Masters in Power Electronics Technology from Shanghai Jiao Tong University. By way of background, until around the 1990s or early 2000s, being a business or trade person was not a prestigious profession in China. The nation had had a communist command economy between the 1940s and 1970s, with private ownership of a business not legalized until 1978. Additionally, Chinese society has the concept of "Four Occupations" of the *fengjian* social structure, the four being: *shi* (gentry scholars), *nong* (peasant farmers), the *gong* (artisans and craftsmen) and the *shang* (merchants and traders). The *shang* had lower status than the *shi*. The successful entrepreneurs in the years following liberalization – the *shang* of the 1980s and 1990s – were often from modest backgrounds and had turned to business out of necessity. Such a subtle prejudice against business people has largely ended since the rise of the billionaire class and celebrity tech entrepreneurs like Jack Ma, but this was not the case in the 1990s. This background helps to explain why the prospect of Zhongqun Mao, the son of the founder, returning from his PhD studies in the USA to take up a role in a family business, would not have been seen as being obviously prestigious or lucrative. He could have had the option of being a senior lecturer at a university, in China or the USA.

Creative Tension and Succession

Initially, he was reluctant to come back and help his father. After he graduated from his postgraduate qualification, he worked in the business for three months. He realized that his parents were struggling. At a family meeting, his father asked him to help, but acknowledged that it was his choice. Given his father's need, and the son's high level of education and career options, Zhongqun was able to specify his requirements. He made three conditions: that he would discontinue the lighter business, as he saw no prospects for growth; that he would not take on employees from the existing factories, but would hire a new workforce; and that the new factory would be in the city, rather than a rural location. Lixiang accepted all conditions.

For six months, Zhongqun, the son, did nothing but research, focusing on electrical goods and automation. China was in a phase of rapid industrialization and growth, but he spotted an opportunity in kitchen appliances. In particular, he noticed that Chinese kitchens were less modernized than in Japan and, given the popularity of sauces in Chinese cuisine, there was a rising demand for cooker hoods. He persuaded his father to invest in such a product, arguing that they would be more profitable than microwaves, his father's preference. Zhongqun also insisted on using the brand name FOTILE, replacing Feixiang. The investment, and the risk, were considerable, but ultimately paid off. It was not a completely immature market: there were over 250 kitchen range hood companies in China, including established brands like BOSS and ZhengTai. Zhongqun led a research team to develop new types of kitchen range hoods. Eight months later, he developed a China's first self-designed large arc streamline hood. The hoods proved very popular and, through excellence in engineering and design, the family were able to maintain a premium price. Zhongqun hired the best specialists, and the firm gained international quality standards including ISO9001. The firm later diversified into a wider range of kitchen fittings.

As an *exit role*, Lixiang set up a college, a business school specializing in family firms. At his college, Lixiang has advised on family ownership, often recommending a diluted family control system. He teaches that the roles of owner and leader should be understood as distinct, and typically separated, owing to the potential for conflicts and lack of expertise. There are classes on directorship, family councils and the role of the CEO. He has written books on the subject, and invites visiting professors to the college. The college also advises on best practices on ownership succession and use of family councils. It is in the region of Ningbo, where Cixi is situated. Students come from all over China, and it accommodates around 300 at any one time. It has become a specialist in serving the manufacturing industry.

9.4 Values and Emotional Ties as Leadership Logic

Cases in this book illustrate how family values, and long-term perspectives, can create a leadership logic that leads to long-term mandates, while maintaining entrepreneurial flair. The Israel tourism business described earlier and the Chinese FOTILE case above are examples of families setting up new ventures that become a part of their values, leadership logic and identity. Strong values are a result of owners learning and are a strategy for what works over a long time for the family, their ownership and business(es). Family values are used to balance short- and long-term considerations when making decisions that affect the profit of the business short term but might benefit the family and ownership long term. The formulation of values will in family ownership be deeply held and often discussed, as so many other things, in the informal domain. The change of such values, as a consequence of new generations, social change or technological development, might trigger revisiting and changing such values. The sustainability and circular economy movement is just such a new political movement that many in the new generation of owners, and employees and leaders, feel very strongly about and identify with. It brings with it a new set of values that will influence the evolutions of ownership and new incubation options.

The family owner might need to revisit, change or adhere to values and it creates tension. In the same way, competing for one top leadership role creates other conflicts. Families strategize for the short and long term so as to secure the family's autonomy, often by creating an increased array of options. In this way, the values and emotional ties are often, through stories or value statements, the leadership logic of the family's owner. In the case of the Israeli family, the strategic value question can be framed as: How do we ensure that our purpose, and values expressed in it, is to be a non-sectarian employer in the pilgrimage tourism service creating safe and informative vacations? Further: How do we implement a leadership based on our value of equality, hence a purpose of resisting the political fragmentation in Israel, so as to demonstrate how members from different religious communities can work together? In addition they would seek financial profit from their activities.

Most entrepreneurs call the process of generating new ideas, discharging bad ones, linking up ideas so they evolve into a concept and from there develop into a venture a roller coaster. A family member or group that ventures into such an emotional roller coaster has strong emotional ties within the family as protective shield. The tension within the family can be tolerated as one tries not to break bonds while arguing or discussing. In the case of selling or letting go of roles or products the emotional ties make family members mourning this as a loss feel supported and cared for.

The family as ownership group will represent certain family values that can evolve over time. It is important not to ignore siblinghood and intragenerational dynamics. Some research has shown that a strong sibling team creates a "we-feeling", and that this can be a crucial motivational factor in building a family firm. Much focus in the psychodynamic field is on the parent–child relationship, and much has a tendency to be slanted towards conflict and rivalry. The potential for powerful team-building by close siblings is comparatively under-researched and under-appreciated. Our research confirms that it possesses huge potential, but of course relationships have to be carefully nurtured and sustained. Psychoanalyst Coles focuses on siblinghood and the development of a "we-sense" between siblings (Osnes, 2016). She points out that these relationships can be significant in the development of individuals and their later relationships, their sense of self and their capacity to trust. One extensive review of unique aspects of successful family businesses concluded that they prioritize building and maintaining socio-emotional wealth for the family. It is a much broader agenda than reaching commercial objectives for a particular business. It covers social identity, maintaining family ties, and, combined with standard business strategies, contributes to entrepreneurial flair and building long-term strategies. The "we identity" of siblings, and not only intergenerational relationships, appears to be an important building block in creating socio-emotional wealth.

9.5 Family Offices

Family offices are often developed from a family council where the family as owners manage family dynamics, long-term strategies and leadership succession. If the family is financially successful, the setting up of a family office can become an important part of the family's ownership strategy and succession plan. Often it can be family members not interested in finance or business who need help to manage their wealth; possibly because they have other careers taking up their time. Initially the office often employs individuals with investment expertise. Family members might be more interested in investments than leading an operational business as CEO, in which case the family office offers a career option. A new generation might decide not to be involved in the main business, but do require help managing their wealth. Family offices centralize management of the family assets, and its financial resources come from the family's company or companies. Wealth may have been built up over generations. The services provided can range from traditional personal services such as concierges, security, insurance and estate planning, to investments in venture capital. The family must have a high net wealth enabling it to take on the costs, and hire the management expertise necessary, to set up a family office. When financial resources increase in value, it makes sense to employ one's own investment team rather than having banks, with high fees, manage the wealth.

Such new types of structures, initially flexible before becoming more fixed structures, are increasingly used for a family to create new roles that can influence the family and succession process. Family members can gravitate toward other types of active roles such as investors starting new ventures, social entrepreneurship and philanthropic activities, often maintaining and developing the family's values and knowledge. In some best practice cases families use the family office to create an educational centre for next generations as well as incubate new ventures. Family offices can create such a transitional space for families (Chapter 2) for experimenting and discussing new ideas. They can tolerate a degree of business failure if there is learning involved. With the development of skills, and repeated execution of certain strategies, an organization or family builds a broader strategic capacity. In the context of a highly enterprising business-owning family, this becomes an intergenerational process. The transmission of knowledge from the older generation to the younger generations consists not only of the knowledge about a particular business, but also involves mutual development and learning, building strategic capacities.

Practice Summary

Sometimes the lessons are best illustrated with story and the FOTILE Chinese case shows the creation of both distributed and monolithic leadership structures, incubation of new enterprises and an innovative exit role for a senior family owner. It illustrates serial entrepreneurship, with the founder setting up a company with his daughter. Later, the son was to take over the main business, with his sister in a minority shareholder role, and the father develop an exit role. The main founder worked throughout his life with his wife, who held an informal leadership role, which is quite typical for women in family firms, though not fully researched or acknowledged. At the time of writing she was still involved in the business, which had developed a distributed leadership system, with the family council helping to keep the family and the enterprises together.

For family owners and their advisors, or non-family leaders, it is important to engage in discussions aimed at reducing conflict around succession. It can help to challenge certain fixed identities with the business. Family councils are often set up so as to manage the family dynamic around succession more generally, to discuss possible new ventures or be the birth-place for family offices. Fixed identities, as described in Chapter 7, can have shadows and unused opportunities. Serial entrepreneurship and new ventures will often challenge a fixation with the original business that triggers rivalry. New ventures often leverage on the main business and in this way an identity to the family business is kept while also creating something new.

Some of the successful business-owning families in my research showed considerable ingenuity and flexibility. They may have used succession as a transfer of business assets (ownership and leadership roles) and succession as a handover of opportunity (new leadership and ownership roles); they could switch between these two strategies or use them concurrently. Succession options that should be discussed are distribution of top leadership roles between family members based on complementary skills and active ownership roles in combination with a hired Managing Director.

References

Gersick, K. E., Davis, J. A., Hampton, M. M., & Lansberg, I. (1997). *Generation to generation: Life cycles of the family business.* Harvard Business Press.

Gronn, P. (2017). Configured leadership. *Encyclopedia of Educational Philosophy and Theory*, 1–6.

Haug, M. (2016). Gender in Family Entrepreneurship. In G. Osnes (Ed.), *Family Capitalism: Best Practices in Ownership and Leadership*, 150.

Lindgren, H. (2002). Succession Strategies in a Large Family Business Group: The Case of the Swedish Wallenberg Family. In *Sixth European Business History Association Annual Congress, Helsinki*.

Michael-Tsabari, N., Labaki, R., & Zachary, R. K. (2014). Toward the cluster model: The family firm's entrepreneurial behavior over generations. *Family Business Review*, 27(2), 161–185.

Osnes, G. (2016). Strategizing successions: Sibling loyalty in a French case. In G. Osnes (Ed.), *Family Capitalism: Best Practices in Ownership and Leadership* (pp. 56–67). Routledge.

Simon, B. (2016). The Nespresso story you never knew, *Business Report*, 27 August 2016. doi:10.1016/j.leaqua.2005.09.005.

10

AUTHORITY AND POWER

It is often said that power corrupts, followed by absolute power corrupts absolutely. This underlines the importance of accountability. While the maxim is generally true, some clarification is needed around the terms that can be used to describe what enables one person to influence another – namely, authority and power. I will make some distinctions between the terms as they are elusive and often conflated or used interchangeably. I will use them as different concepts for influence as it is important for understanding succession. Thereby, the focus in this chapter is what will be seen as legitimate power and what will be given, or can be earned, of authority. At the heart of a succession process, and in understanding the influence of leadership, lies the granting of executive discretion. Executive discretion will mean the degrees of freedom a leader has in decision making and accountability. All governance regulations giving executive discretion, and systems for CEO accountability, are just frameworks; executive discretion should addressed by the governance body, negotiated and agreed with the incoming leader.

Hype surrounding celebrity CEOs has created an impression of unbridled power and it can be misleading. The CEO's power should be temporary, defined and contextual. Power, as we often think about it, disappears without trust among shareholders, under the pressure from shareholders and the stakeholder community. Within the fields of leadership and governance one often uses the term executive discretion so as to capture the degree of freedom a top leader or CEO has. Even if it seems an obvious point, any misunderstanding within the board and with the CEO with regards to executive discretion can lead to destructive tension. It follows that a new CEO should be cautious in assuming he will have the same degrees of freedom that the predecessor had. A CEO entry and executive authority will depend on several factors. To avoid conflict a strong mandate has to be seen, together with the confidence a board has in the succession pool, and how much authority a new leader brings from earlier performance. The ambition of the board members and the chair, and the competence of the board, will also matter.

Many other types of organizations might have different governing bodies, or different logics on leadership. All structures need to suit the unique context and a very specific task or purpose, such as in the Vatican case described in Chapter 6. The logic on leadership will evolve if the organization's task, or a wider purpose, is necessary. As such I argue for a process of making the succession a strategic event but will suggest one is pragmatic with regards to what is an ideal logic on leadership. In the boxes throughout the book we share historical cases showing how leadership logic, and succession strategies ensuring a leadership logic, are harboured in succession and will influence the outcome of each of the succession strategies. Despite the differences there are also very different degrees of discretion given within the different types of organizations and their stakeholders and across cultures (Crossland & Hambrick, 2007). Through history, the amount of freedom or power given has always been debated, from the ancient area in Greece and Rome to today's discussion when one compares different regulative frameworks or the difference between family- and non-family-owed businesses.

In the following section I will elaborate on executive discretion and what is often meant by authority and the wielding of power. I discuss the significance of the role difference between the USA, which often features duality of role, and European governance practices. I describe how family owners successfully and consciously can manage such processes. Alibaba, at the time of writing the largest online retailer in the world, offers an example of such evolution in their governance structure, and how this was negotiated at the stock market in New York and Hong Kong. I will describe the hybrid governance system of Alibaba set in place at a juncture where founder Jack Ma was exiting the top leadership role. This is seen in context with other trends in how to manage the powers, and executive authority, inherent in succession processes.

10.1 Executive Discretion

What a governance structure does, through a succession process, is to give a leader executive discretion. It is defining what degrees of freedom the top leader has without consulting the board. One should not assume that the CEO's discretion is the same at each company, or the same before and after a succession within the same company. At the entry of a new CEO there will be assumptions before the entry, and in the immersion into the role, of the necessary level of executive discretion. In certain circumstances the board may need to step in to prevent a vacuum. In Chapter 3 I discuss the lame duck period and how a board might step in before a CEO exits and a new CEO takes up the role.

Executive discretion given will be different across cultures and organizations. The concept of managerial discretion has been the subject of academic research and inquiry since at least the 1930s. From early studies on executive behaviour to more recent empirical studies on executive effects (Sanders, 2001), it has been assumed in much research that senior leaders have significant influence on organizational performance. Scholars have attempted to analyse not only the degree to which managers have discretion, but what this has meant for organizational outcomes, and in which ways. Researchers Hambrick and Finkelstein analysed three levels; the incoming leader's political acumen and personal influence, the governance system's influence and the context in terms of dynamics and regulation (Hambrick & Finkelstein, 1987).

One of the problems with knowing, and comparing, how much CEOs matter is bound up in differences in discretion. The amount of influence, prestige and privilege given to leaders varies widely by culture. In some cultures, there are severe constraints on what leaders can and cannot do. In other cultures, leaders are granted a substantial amount of power over followers and are given special privileges and high status. One study provided strong evidence that, in line with expectation, CEOs in the USA had considerably greater discretion and authority than in Germany, with its two-tier board system and ban on combined CEO-chair role, and Japan (Crossland & Hambrick, 2007). While widely dispersed shareholdings, such as in the USA, would appear to be consistent with an entrepreneurial culture and greater executive discretion, there are two major caveats. Firstly, studies that have confirmed such a correlation are historic, and such dynamics are in a state of flux. Secondly, the extent to which enterprising families become significant incubators could cause the correlation to weaken, or even break down.

10.2 Authority and Power

Authority builds on, and comes with, executive discretion. A leader will carry with them some authority from being chosen. Authority, for a new top leader, might be something one brings with oneself, or develops when in the role. One can also by reputation have personal authority. One can have authority by earning it through performance. The term authority also describes the knowledge, personal presence and competence of a person. A new CEO can be seen as having a great deal of personal authority, but it has to be seen as relevant for the organization, and the board, for it to be authority one actually exerts in the role. The board and the incoming CEO have to be level-headed, as this is the realm where an over-idealization of a leader, possibly as part of a group dynamic where an elite is reproducing itself, or individual narcissism, might confuse the succession process (see Chapters 4 and 5). A sense of having to prove oneself, and gain an organization's trust, is often expressed as important in the entry process. Authority is a healthy feature of leadership and the result of a negotiated process that might be ongoing throughout the tenure. It can be frustrating but the best remedy for hubris, groupthink or that top leaders become too narcissistic is to have a strong focus on negotiating authority. I have over the years often had to coach top leaders who have started to become too narcissistic as the employees and other leaders, or the company, will suffer. A growth sector where the actual competence or leadership skill might be less crucial might buffer, or disguise, the negative effects of narcissistic leadership.

There may be a difference between the powers one is attributed with, compared with the executive authority given, or the authority one conveys through performance. Power is a more elusive term. It has some elasticity in its definition, as it is used to denote the influence of someone that is one or all of the following; broad and impactful or unchecked. It is often rather political in its usage. Often when someone talks about a leader as powerful it has a connotation of awe or fear. We are often referring to our own subjective experiences when describing someone as being powerful. It is often in relationship to how the individual can influence our lives in a positive or negative way. It refers to a subjective feeling around our sense of control and how others can facilitate or reduce this. Many leaders who enter into a CEO role for the first time comment on how people in the organization begin relating to them in a different way. On entry into a top leadership role a CEO is learning how to use the executive discretion given, with accountability, to build personal authority and trust within the organization. The actual power a CEO wields, based on executive discretion and personal authority, is an important ongoing consideration for the board. It may differ from that which is anticipated and can shift during the tenure of the leader. A leader being seen as or managing to become indispensable is always giving that individual, when it lasts for some time, too much power.

BOX 10.1 THE ARMOUR OF ACHILLES

By Agnes Wilhelmsen

Armor and shields were a fundamental necessity in. We see their significance and symbolic meaning in the series of epics revolving around the events before, during and after the Trojan war (as described in *The Iliad*, *The Odyssey*, *The Aeneid*, and *Philoctetes*). Auctoritas is the Latin word that formed the etymological root of authority, and was by Greek writers symbolized as armor and shields. The shield or armour was used to reference an individual's military prowess, their lineage and finally their successor. Shields/armour, as the auctoritas term later, was something a person wore — it can be given but one must be worthy. It also has to be used. In *The Iliad*, an ancient Greek poem, we will see three claims, or entitlements, to auctoritas/authority that are also present today.

In *The Iliad*, describing the Trojan war between the Greeks and Troy, we see how symbolically powerful armour was. The hero is Achilles and he is the symbol of authority. Throughout the poem there are stories that show shifts in power, legitimacy and entitlement. Patroclus, Achilles' friend and possibly his lover, borrows Achilles' armour and uses it in the fighting. (Achilles spends quite a bit the years of the war sulking in his tent.)

Homer describes the following:

> When the Trojans saw strong Patroclus and his attendant Automedon beside him in all their brilliance of their bronze armour, panic threatened and the ranks began to waver, since they thought swift-footed Achilles must have abandoned his anger and reconciled himself with Agamemnon. Every man looked anxiously around to find some escape from sudden death.

(Homer, 2003)

Source: *Alamy*

Patroclus is killed by Hector, the Prince of Troy, and Achilles' armour and shield are lost. In grief and anger Achilles, at last some would say, decides to fight. Thetis (Achilles' mother) has influence among the gods and Hephaestus, an Olympian god, makes her son new armour and shield thereby enforcing armour's symbol as auctoritas based on military prowess and distinguished lineage. Achilles' shield is described as depicting an artistic microcosm of civilization featuring a city in peacetime, a city at war and another city, along with illustrations of the sun, moon and ocean.

Achilles is killed by Paris, shot in the heel. A trial, and election, is set up among the Greek forces to decide who will be his successor and be given his armour. The competitors are Ajax and Odysseus. Ajax is known as being an outstanding warrior, second to none but Achilles himself. Courage and honour present him as the rightful heir by tradition. However, Odysseus' masterful utilization of rhetoric and genius in manipulative military tactics makes the armour awarded to him. Ajax goes mad and commits suicide.

Another aspect of this story is suggested in the Sophocles tragedy *Philoctetes* performed in 409 BCE. Neoptolemus, Achilles' son, arrives on the scene at Troy demanding his father's armour by right as his son. Agamemnon, leader of the Greek army, refuses. Odysseus is rewarded the armour in a succession based on an election rather than inheritance.

Auctoritas (Roman) and armour/shields (Greek) and what it is to get it and have it are symbolized in different ways. Ajax symbolizes the traditionally noble Homeric hero that Achilles encapsulated. In Homer's *The Odyssey* and *The Iliad* Odysseus is supported by the goddess of wisdom, Athene, and is instrumental in devising the scheme around the Trojan horse. Sophocles expands on the Homeric hero's unique set of skills by portraying him as a political animal clever rather than brave, manipulative but still effective. A shift is emphasized, through the story, toward an electoral system of government, susceptible to powers of rhetoric and individual talent. It is at the expense of morality, dismissing the rightful heir, Ajax, for a more dynamic successor, Odysseus.

Achilles' armour bears profound auctoritas. The Romans would later develop and use auctoritas as a term pertaining in particular to the Roman senate. In Rome an individual could possess auctoritas depending on their prestige and ability to gather support and align it to their purpose. The term bears political but also divine significance in the individual's power of command.

10.3 Role Duality and Non-duality

Executive discretion and power evolve around governance designs with regards to the leadership of a board and the CEO role. Use of role duality, the same person having both roles, and non-duality, where there are different leaders in each role, can be seen in different cultures and types of organizations. In the USA and Europe different understandings of best practices have resulted in different levels of executive discretion. In the USA, the roles of chair and CEO are often combined, whereas this is specifically prohibited in Germany and Scandinavia. Non-duality implies that the distinction between the CEO and chair roles is made clearer in Europe, especially continental Europe, than in the USA. The purpose of separating the roles is to reduce discretion and the risk of hubris. In the museum case (see Chapter 8), the introduction of a CEO role was supported by the concept of non-duality.

The decision of whether to opt for duality affects the balance of power between the board and CEO. It is also linked to the question of whether there is an executive group and a board. In continental Europe, there is typically a two-tier system that holds the potential for greater clarity and distinction between executive and directorial responsibilities, and there is more compulsion for privately owned companies to appoint a board. Germany's two-tier system features a supervisory and a management board, and, as in Scandinavia, mandatory employee representation. In the USA, where there is often duality, it is generally seen as necessary to have powerful independent board members and a strong nominations committee to oversee the succession. Even with such measures, the practice nonetheless still grants considerable power to one individual, and muddies the waters around the governing versus executive roles.

In Japan, the board is comparatively less powerful and features many executives, but the keiretsu system involves a close network of cross-shareholdings that exert control over executive discretion. The UK's system lies somewhere in between, with a unitary board comprising non-executives and executives, but codes of guidance that strongly condemn a combined CEO–chair role, as part of a comply or explain regime.

The trend has been to move away from combining the roles of CEO and chair – a development that bruises the egos of founders and top leaders alike. In October 2019 Dennis Muilenburg was removed as chair of the board of the aerospace giant Boeing, but remained as CEO. This followed a period in which the company had faced controversy over features of its 737 MAX design, blamed for two fatal crashes following which the aircraft had been grounded. In 2018 Elon Musk had given up the chairmanship of Tesla, the technology firm he had founded. The change followed an investigation by the Securities & Exchange Commission into messages he had posted on Twitter speculating about changes in ownership. Again, he remained as chief executive. This was part of a trend: The Economist reported in October 2019 that the number of combined roles in the S&P 500 companies had fallen by almost a half since 2001.

The common career path of operational executive to chief executive to chair of the board rings alarm bells. The particular career path of CEO-to-chair is a warning indicator if it becomes institutionalized. In Chapter 11 a case shows what risks such trajectories pose. It can also be an indicator of lack of diversity, elite preservation and even collusion over malpractice.

The move towards far greater representation of women, and people who are not from the white male population who have dominated board representation across much of the corporate world, is an additional reason for separation of role, creating a representative population at senior levels, rather than a clique of individuals from a similar background with similar perspectives.

Embedded in the questions about duality/non-duality of role, and executive discretion, a two-tier system enables some monitoring of the CEO and accountability while also maintaining unity of command. To be able to monitor and keep a CEO accountable it is, in Europe, seen as crucial that the board has independence. Independence cannot be assured simply by citing the design and proportion of non-executives; there is also a concept of independence of mind and judgement. Quality of experience and guidance, and the strength of the relationships – qualitative issues that cannot be gauged from a distance or through benchmarks – are ultimately what shape performance. If duality in the role becomes problematic it can be can be counteracted by designating a board member as Lead Director. Within the board, possibly supported by a nomination committee, one is in this way enabling more independence from the CEO. There are significant differences between corporations and family businesses; the latter can choose to fail in one business, deciding to invest in another. Their ultimate loyalty is to the family, rather than a single institution. This gives the wealthy owning family immense power and autonomy.

10.4 Alibaba: Succeeding Jack Ma

Nearly two decades on from the celebrated, and ultimately underwhelming, handover from Jack Welch to Jeff Immelt at GE, a similarly well-telegraphed, and anticipated, succession was announced by the Chinese billionaire Jack Ma, founder of Alibaba. He and his team had built and grown the online retail behemoth since its launch in 1999. He was originally a teacher of English and a translator. He was born Ma Yun in Hangzhou, south eastern China, in 1964 during communist rule. His family was not wealthy or well connected, but following President Nixon's visit to Hangzhou during his historic trip to China in 1972, the town began attracting Western tourists, and Ma Yun quickly learned English and would offer them tours, gaining the nickname Jack.

In the 1990s, after a visit to the USA, he spotted the potential of the internet to enable people to buy and sell products and services directly and internationally. Alibaba was his third attempt at setting up an internet company. He founded it with 17 friends, initially offering Chinese companies the opportunity to post product listings, from which customers could buy directly. The site gained popularity quickly, enabling him to attract investment capital, which funded further growth. In 2005 the Silicon Valley giant Yahoo invested $1 billion in Alibaba in exchange for a 40% stake, which proved to be an immensely profitable deal for both sides. By 2013, Alibaba's ecommerce companies registered a higher turnover than Amazon and eBay combined. Jack Ma was CEO throughout the early years of expansion, stepping down as CEO in 2013 but staying as chair of the board.

Alibaba prepared for a public listing with an unusual governance arrangement, as Ma wanted a hybrid structure with control over appointment of board members retained by founders, who were still managers at the company. It was initially rejected in Hong Kong, operating a principle of one share one vote, as shareholders would not have had control over the appointment of the CEO. This was an understandable reaction, given the principle of separation of governance and executive, but due to the scale of the listing it was controversial. There is a track record of technology companies gaining a listing where the founder retains significant control, for example through super-voting shares (Townsend, 2017), but the legal and regulatory systems are different respectively in Hong Kong and the USA (Cheng, 2014). Listing was subsequently approved in New York in March 2014, and at $150 billion Alibaba became the biggest IPO in the history of the New York Stock Exchange. Hong Kong was judged to have missed out to the New York stock-market on a lucrative and prestigious listing, as the listing would have benefited the economy and boosted the reputation of Hong Kong as a financial centre. Jack Ma became the wealthiest person in China, with the listing netting him $25 billion. He moved from the post of CEO to become executive chairman (D'Onfro & Stone, 2014). There was a subsequent listing in Hong Kong.

10.5 Emerging Governance Systems

An increasing trend with how family owners use a family office to incubate new ventures rather than hand over a company to one family member, also possible in partnership with non-family actors, This accentuates how it is important to explore, and have ingenuity, in how one develops governance systems. I have explored the monolithic and distributed ownership and leadership systems emerging, or often ignored, in family ownership. I discussed if social trends such as gender, and a focus on other stakeholders, lead to hybrid or new types of governance systems for a business and organization. At the same time, some tech firms have developed hybrid governance systems. At Alibaba after the listing, Jack Ma and management owned only 10% of the shares but controlled the board and had majority voting rights (Cheng, 2014). This is similar to super-voting rights at large USA tech firms. The set up would appear to combine the apparent advantages of private and public ownership simultaneously, but it may not retain its popularity if performance dips and shareholders become discontented. In common with other tech companies, the founder group at Alibaba retains significant control, with a view to maintaining the company's values and ethos, and balancing potential short-term interests of institutional and activist investors with a longer term perspective. Alibaba's founder group has developed a unique partnership mechanism.

Alibaba's initial group of partners numbered 30. In 2015 and 2017, four new partners were added, while in August 2016, Lu Zhaojun and Jiang Peng announced their retirement and became honorary partners without partnership rights. The Alibaba Partner Committee is a smaller, select group of partners that oversees day-to-day management. At November 2019, there were five members, according to the company website: Jack Ma, Joe Tsai, Daniel Zhang, Lucy Peng and Eric Jing. Jack Ma wrote an open letter about Alibaba's Partner Committee saying: 'What sets our partnership apart from the others is that this is not a mere profit sharing mechanism, nor is it a vehicle of power to exert greater control over the company: rather, it is a system that provides a driving force within the company. This system will help inculcate Alibaba Group's mission, vision and values, safeguard the culture of innovation, improve our organization, enable us to become more nimble and competitive in the future, and help us to create our ideal future. At the same time, we also hope that the partnership system, operating based on a foundation of transparency, can shield the company's long-range development plans from the short-term profit seeking trends of the capital market. With that, we hope to provide all shareholders with greater long-term returns' (www.alizila.com/alibaba-groups-ma-explains-his-companys-unusual-partnership-system). Partner numbers are adjusted each year, with a nomination and election process. There are no quota restrictions, but conditions are strict. Partners must show integrity and have at least five years' experience with the company. They need to have made an outstanding contribution to the group, and obtain a 75% agreement from current partners.

In September 2018, Jack Ma prepared for a further significant move, as he announced the succession for the role as executive chair. He announced that Daniel Zhang, at the time the CEO, would succeed him exactly a year later. Jack Ma was effectively retiring from active involvement in Alibaba. In his eloquent and thoughtful statement at the time of the announcement on the succession, he made an intriguing reference to his background as a teacher, comparing this role to the succession task:

> Teachers always want their students to exceed them, so the responsible thing for me and the company to do is to let younger, more talented people take over in leadership roles so that they inherit our mission "to make it easy to do business anywhere."
>
> The partnership system we developed is a creative solution to good governance and sustainability, as it overcomes several challenges faced by companies of scale: continuous innovation, leadership succession, accountability and cultural continuity. Over the years, in iterating our management model, we have experimented with and improved on the right balance between systems and individuals. Simply relying on individuals or blindly following a system will not solve our problems. To achieve long-term sustainable growth, you need the right balance among system, people and culture. I have full confidence that our partnership system and efforts to safeguard our culture will in time win over the love and support from customers, employees and shareholders.
>
> (Kelly, 2019)

As a statement of good practice on governance, succession and maintaining values and an innovative culture, it could not be improved upon. The real test, however, is in implementing and honouring the principles. The longer term outcome was not clear at the time of writing, just a year after the announcement and a few weeks after the handover.

Practice Summary

Within a business context board members should set themselves in the back seat. Governance is about care and stewardship; it is far more than a regulatory function meeting legal and financial requirements. I advocate, regardless of the type of governance design, that the governing function's legitimacy is bound up in its capacity to trigger or create succession outcomes. To be able to have this capacity the board monitors the financial well being of the company, has discussions with the CEO, shareholders and other stakeholders. If trust in the CEO is lost, based on these functions, the board's duty is to trigger a succession. The chapter discussed how authority and power are managed and created.. Within family-owned companies there is often a small group of shareholders who control this wielding of power more closely than shareholders on the stock market.

For family owners and their advisors, or non-family leaders, it is important to trigger other types of discussion that can reduce conflict around succession, while challenging certain fixed identities with the business. Family councils are often set up to manage the family dynamic around succession more generally, to discuss possible new ventures or be the birthplace for family offices. Fixed identities, as described in Chapter 7, can have shadows and unused opportunities. Serial entrepreneurship and new ventures will often challenge a fixation with the original business that triggers rivalry. New ventures often leverage on the main business and in this way the identity of the family business is kept while also creating something new.

Some of the successful business-owning families in my research showed considerable ingenuity and flexibility. They have used succession as a transfer of business assets (ownership and leadership roles) and as a hand-over of opportunity (new leadership and ownership roles); they could switch between these two strategies or use them concurrently. Succession options that should be discussed are the distribution of top leadership roles between family members based on complementary skills or active ownership roles in combination with a hired Managing Director. Different distributed ownership structures can be developed that attend to business challenges, family talents and motivation. Incubation as a succession strategy includes new ventures and cluster ownership, as well as serial entrepreneurship where the family builds new ventures and sells old ones. The family office may operate as a learning resource and new venture incubator. Some options, such as serial entrepreneurship, might suit new family owners in the first and second generation. When the family is becoming experienced in business development, they can develop a cluster of companies. With increased wealth, they can use a family office. These incubation strategies ease the classic family rivalry and can be done together with or instead of distributed or monolithic succession strategies. In the latter case, when families employ CEOs, the succession strategies described in Chapter 3 are useful.

References

Cheng, A. T. (2014). Alibaba IPO stirs listing rules debate in Hong Kong. *Institutional Investor*, 14 July 2014.

Crossland, C., & Hambrick, D. C. (2007). How national systems differ in their constraints on corporate executives: A study of CEO effects in three countries. *Strategic Management Journal*, 28(8), 767–789.

D'Onfro, J., & Stone, M. (2014). The inspiring life story of Alibaba founder Jack Ma, *Business Insider*, 2 October 2014.

Hambrick, D. C., & Finkelstein, S. (1987). Managerial discretion: A bridge between polar views of organizational outcomes. *Research in Organizational Behavior*, 9, 369–406.

Kelly, J. (2019). From Poor Beginnings to Billionaire Status: Jack Ma Retires from Alibaba. *Forbes*, 10 September 2019.

Sanders, W. G. (2001). Behavioral responses of CEOs to stock ownership and stock option pay, *Academy of Management Journal*, 44(3), 447–492.

Townsend, T. (2017, June 13). Alphabet shareholders want more voting rights but Larry and Sergey don't want it that way, *Vox.com*.

11

THE BOARD: TRUST AND FOLLOWERSHIP

An organization, to function well, fundamentally relies on trust. Trust is crucial between the board and CEO, between a CEO and the leadership team, other employees, shareholders and other stakeholders. Lack of trust is often, in daily use, referred to as a toxic work environment or relationship. It can have many unhealthy origins and a lack of trust in the top of the organization is one of them. With distrust comes mutual suspicion, safeguarding of interest, speculation in private, informal alliances and increasing degrees of power politics. During my career I have encountered employees or leaders who feel they are, due to such a toxic environment, unable to enjoy their work, relax or cooperate effectively with colleagues. They are always on their guard and it is a very unhealthy and destructive type of stress. On contrast trust encompasses a sense of hope: setting out a future that is ambitious but plausible, based on an understanding of the past and the inherent strengths of the organization. Hope does not need to be grand – it can result from a good week where one had rewarding achievements to more wider ambitions of fun, interesting work and success.

For the new CEO the entry process is the start of establishing mutual trust within the organization in addition to building on what he/she has with the board. The nebulous but crucial dimension of trust in an organ-izational context has been the subject of considerable academic inquiry. Studies have demonstrated how a high level of trust results in more posi-tive workplace behaviours, attitudes, better team processes and superior levels of performance. It is likely to encourage innovation. After decades of research, a discernible consensus emerged in the 1990s around how trust can be conceptualized and identified. There is an understanding that trust is a psychological state comprising two vital, and interrelated, elem-ents: a preparedness for vulnerability and positive expectations (Fulmer and Gelfand, 2012).

In the following I explore trust as it is the crucial, but elusive, trigger of a succession or result of a well managed succession and entry process. I use a case to illustrate how bad successions can lead to the collapse of trust and will describe how the integration of succession practices creates trust or distrust. The board has a care function that is the basis for the trust given to the CEO and is the basis for the establishment of followership within the organization. Throughout this chapter I will describe how trust in organizations is important and how the integration of succession strat-egies contributes to such trust. I will use a case where trust had eroded owing to a CEO-to-chair career trajectory that led to a CEO revolving door and firing of the chair. I will also discuss care as a duty of boards and the subject of followership.

11.1 Trust

An academic who has studied the nature of trust in human relationships is Ana Cristina Costa of Brunel University London. She emphasizes that trust between individuals is not static; it can build, decline and renew itself based on individuals' prior experience, propensity to trust and how relationships develop (Costa et al., 2018). Based on her research, and the work of others, three types of trust have been identified: calculus-based, knowledge-based and identification-based. Calculus-based trust is the type formed early in relationship-building, where individuals make the assessment that there is mutual advantage to a trusting relationship and risk of reduced reputation by breaking that trust. Knowledge-based is based on experience gained through a relationship and mutual trust being demonstrated. Identification-based trust is that which derives from closeness of affiliation, shared world-view and values and a shared enterprise. The three types can be experienced as sequential, as phases in a relationship, but there is no guarantee of moving from one to the next. Some formality of agreements, in the way of contracts, can help the move from calculus-based to knowledge-based trust, but ultimately the level of trust established depends upon the quality of relationships.

Here another type of trust will be explored. Trust in the organization is distinct from interpersonal trust one has of colleagues or between board members and the CEO, or between the CEO and leaders. Trust in an organization can rely on such interpersonal trust, but from a board perspective the trust one has in the organization, independent from interpersonal trust, is something different. Nurturing trust to the organization is the overriding objective of how boards strategize and authorize a top leader. With regards to the entry of a new CEO, the way the succession has been handled, and the trust one has to the board, is fundamental for trust on the part of stakeholders. Stakeholders include employees and other leaders in the organization whose retention and motivation, in a knowledge- and skill-based economy, is crucial.

Organizational Trust

Trust is about predictability and that key interests will be safeguarded, such as employees' salaries, career opportunities and organizational needs. Blind trust is a concept reflecting a wishful, uncritical state of mind. In an organizational sense there are so many interests it would be naïve to have blind trust. At the other extreme consistent distrust is a form of cynicism likely to result in a self-fulfilling state of disillusionment. A balanced view is informed by review and monitoring of leaders. In this sense a failed succession, or a succession process that seems compromised or not adaptive, could be seen as a warning sign. There will always be gossip in the workforce or among shareholders about leadership, questions such as: Is this a legitimate leadership regime? Is the board independent?

Trust is central to human life. Its importance to workplace and societal relationships has been increasingly the subject of research. In this context there are two broad categories: trust between individuals at the level of working relationships, and wider trust in an institution or social system

(Costa et al., 2018). At the individual psychodynamic level, one's propensity to trust is influenced by early experiences; those with strong bonding and attachments (see Chapter 5) are likely to be more stable and trusting. It is also a factor in the propensity of individuals, leadership groups and wider businesses to tolerate risk. Trust is essential to entrepreneurship; without a certain element of faith that an unproven course of action is likely to prove rewarding, no new initiative would ever be launched. Trust does not, of itself, guarantee risk-taking: it is necessary but not sufficient.

Once trust is lost it can be difficult to restore. One of the most visible representations of forfeited trust in an institution is a run on a bank when depositors, fearing that the bank is becoming insolvent, form a long queue to withdraw their savings before it is too late. All leaders and employees have a blend of different needs and motivations in their work, such as financial, a sense of belonging and identity, to display and develop expertise, to be challenged, to have fun and to show and exercise care for their stakes and the future of their stake and interests in being involved in the organization. Other perfectly valid motivations, including for a top leader, are financial rewards, status and enjoying competition.

11.2 Strategy Integration

Propensity to trust, preparedness for vulnerability and positive expectations to an organization, is shaped by upbringing and experience; most seek a middle way between blind trust and cynicism. Perceived trustworthiness to an organization is multi-dimensional. It can, for limited time periods, rely on the trust one has of others within the organization or of the CEO and other leaders. Fundamentally, personal trust relationships will not counteract trust in the organization if it does not seem to take care of our fundamental needs. As employees and leaders, we expect the organization to harbour ambition. This is done by showing it has ability, benevolence and integrity. A leader must provide this independent of the individual trust he/she has to others. A board safeguards the same feature. It needs to demonstrate:

- Ability – in succession capability and monitoring;
- Benevolence – ability to serve other stakes' interests beyond the members' or board's interests;

- Integrity – capability to monitor in a fair way, and show honest and fair process, not overridden by vested interests or excessive ambition.

A succession is the ultimate stress test for a board and it brings the chair, and the board, into an operative role. Below, building on the Succession Strategy Wheel, is a model showing how stakeholders will monitor trust, based on the how the board, or a CEO appointment, has integrity in its overall narrative (see Figure 11.1).

The term narrative in this context means that there is a strategic thread throughout that makes sense. The board has to have created a mandate for leadership, and the leadership skills should match this as much as possible. Board members willingly, and without elite preservation, use an appropriate pool of candidates. They grant executive authority in a deliberate and reasonable way, concluding a deal that is reasonable and not corrupting. The handover is well managed.

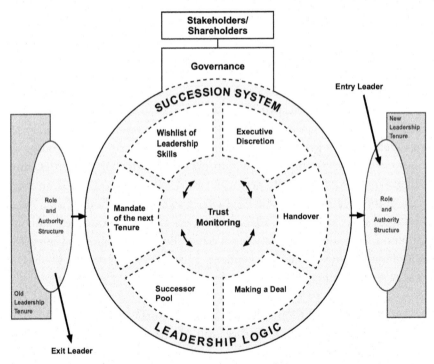

Figure 11.1 Governance, Succession Strategies and Trust-monitoring

The overall framework of legitimacy of a succession system and leadership logic, described in Chapter 6, would be challenged if a board were repeatedly unable to oversee an effective succession. The current debate around women's access to top leadership roles and board roles exemplifies this. The longer women have been out in the workforce, with higher education and long careers, the more questionable it becomes if a big corporation is not able to have an even distribution of men and women in the upper echelon of the business. One could question if there are subjective aspects of what is seen as merit effectively excluding women; biases that keep them out of executive programmes as they happen over weekends, given that women often have more than half of the duty of home making.

Other possible flaws in how succession strategies are compromised can have grave consequences, as shown in the case in the next chapter. Group dynamics such as scapegoating, individual ambition, a hubristic leader staying at the helm and flaws in the monitoring of the boards can all reduce trust. Top leaders and board members should not fool themselves into thinking stakeholders don't notice. A strong leadership ambition from a leader, financial safety in employment, safeguarding pensions investments and personal reputations are strong stakes. When such stakes are at risk, fear and anger create a sense of vigilance and alertness. The mind is hard-wired to make us emotionally react so as to safeguard our needs. Stakeholders can react to miscommunication and wrong information. Any reason for lack of care in succession strategy and integration, be it real or imagined, might be detected and trigger more intense trust monitoring from stakeholders.

11.3 Clean Energy: Collapse of Trust

The company in this case, Clean Energy, was almost driven into bankruptcy by a bad succession practice. In addition there was a total collapse of trust; within the board, between the top leadership and employees to a former chair of the board and also within the organization. These several factors all contributed to this collapse. A chair had been recruited into the role after having been the CEO for many years. He himself recruited a new CEO who left the role very quickly. Due to a troubling financial situation and other factors he was ousted and a new chair recruited. The new chair, Ben, had been in several top leadership roles. He had been in the energy sector throughout his whole career and had been in the role as an external board member for some months. He was asked to become the new chair and as a relatively fresh board member had to grapple with a situation where it was unclear what the financial situation of the company was. It was unclear what had gone wrong in recruiting the former CEO into a chair role and the sudden exit of his predecessor and then the chair himself.

> I knew the business was struggling when I became the chair. I had been at four board meetings and it was not quite clear how the company had so much debt. The chair was elusive and with the departure of the CEO the board got a sense there were issues we did not understand or were given insight to. After some months as chair I found out that the company was almost bust. Bear in mind, this is a business that is in the renewable energy business. It was owned by some local councils and was based on waterfall energy. All the early investments had been done and the market developed. It should technically not be possible for it to fail unless something careless, unethical and illegal was at play. And this was exactly what was the case. Furthermore, the situation had been covered up by the chair for over two years. He had been a CEO and, with some board approval, giving out revenue that was bigger than the profit. In that sense the councils used the company as a cash machine when their budgets had a deficit. Some of the board's external members had represented these councils. When the CEO became the chair, he worked to cover up these practices while also seeking to appoint a new CEO. This was of course not something a CEO with integrity could accept and he rightly resigned. The council has the legal right to ask for dividends. Historically the board and CEO had complied but there was no surplus and the company built up debts. The board was then not acting out its duty to be a caretake of the organization.
>
> The bad practices of giving in to the councils in revenue did breed other types of bad dispositions under the CEO [later chair].
>
> The accumulation of debt was of course highly problematic as it depleted the company and reduced investments in new technology, among other things. What made it a life-threatening situation was how a CEO was allowed to become the chair of the board and by this cover up the problem for two years. It took us three years to sort this out. We managed to recruit an experienced leader from another sector.

There are both short- and long-term risks with letting a CEO go into the chair role of the same company. Short-term risks include the greater likelihood to cover up mistakes or malpractice, with a chair who is likely still to identify with management and may have a reduced monitoring capacity. Individuals can tacitly regard the chair as the real boss, with the CEO as a deputy but it makes it harder to attract the best executive to the top role. When the role of the CEO is slightly diminished in this way, it can lead to overly high expectations of the top executive, and result in over-idealization and consequent frustration.

A long-term risk is that a CEO to chair transition becomes an institutionalized career path within the organization. It is often based on a misunderstanding of the role of the board; that it is an extension of the executive function, whereas its proper role is one of monitoring and care (see Chapter 12 for further discussion). Another long-term risk is linked to how monitoring of the CEO and executives becomes institutionalized, as there is a perception, or a reality, of a single leadership team. It can lead to groupthink that inhibits open discussion and honest appraisal of risk, as well as elite preservation around what becomes a tightly bonded clique. Implications are an arbitrarily narrow field of candidates for the succession and therefore weakened succession capability.

The chair of the board is a role of fundamental importance, and is central to the task of maintaining trust. It is a strategic, non-executive role. A succession in which the CEO moves to become chair often reflects a lack of a proper strategy-based succession process – deployment of the seven strategies described in Chapter 2. It can be that the different threats of group or individual emotional forces, or both in combination, have eroded the different strategies necessary to optimize the succession process. The CEO to chair transition can at the time feel like an easy alternative to a thorough process where several of the strategies are integrated.

11.4 The Care of the Board and Independence

The role of a board is not often discussed as a care function, but care lies at the heart of its responsibilities. Much regulation of boards places an emphasis on clarity of role and independence of at least some board directors from executive duties; this does not go far enough to ensure effective governance. At the heart of the duty is care, and establishing trust in leadership. There are specific legal duties for board members that vary to some degree by jurisdiction. Legal duty is the long-term success and well being of the company, which can be interpreted as a care function. It can be judged to encompass commercial success, sustainability and social responsibility and there are arguments of how and if they can be combined. There have been criticisms of a narrow focus on shareholder returns; a healthy board is able to discuss different priorities and different stakeholder interests.

The role of a board that shows carefulness for the organization should be to provide a space for discussion and to be an enabler rather than a doer. This is a different mindset from being a strong and dynamic top leader seeking profit, growth in people and the company. Of course a board is free to select such a top leader as executive, if appropriate, but there is a significant difference between the executive and a board role. Loss of care can have many different causes. A significant risk is when the board becomes too operational. It can lead to a crowding out of the executive team, or uncritical, even exuberant, support of high-risk strategies by executives. Such dynamics can occur when there is unchecked alpha male ambition. In this way, the board has lost its independence and monitoring capacity. Board directors need to be critical friends, to challenge strategies and the assumptions that underlie them.

The care function is in general an enabling function and ideally only in succession will a board have an executive role; it creates trust in a new leader and trust in the board. As the role of the chair, and the board, are non-executive, they may appear passive, especially from an active, alpha male point of view where influence is equated with activity. But while the role is not to interfere in managerial details, the board does need to be well informed. It also has to be continually vigilant, inquiring and maintaining a keen oversight on the company's affairs. And it may have to act if the leadership fails or stops working. Caring, as in nurturing, means providing some support, safe boundaries and provisions that enable someone or something else to grow or develop. Culturally, and partly biologically, this has been seen as a female function, but in reality it is for both genders and is a central duty of the board. There is a strong case that gender-balanced boards can help maintain balance and effective oversight, though it is not a guarantee.

The Independence Issue

An area of discussion that often emerges concerns how active the board should be in giving specific strategic goals for the CEO. This should become clear when creating the mandate, one of the seven succession strategies. In the case of a family business, the board will be more actively developing the strategy than in many corporations, and the mandate will be more tightly defined. There is a difficulty for the board and chair if they are too active in the formulation of the strategy, as they lose some of their independence in reviewing and monitoring it. The primary task of the board is overall responsibility for ensuring that the top leader is well suited for the strategy and the context.

There is often an emphasis, when defining the role of the board and the chair, on independence from the executive team, as ultimately it has to hold executives to account. A board is the boss of the CEO, not a colleague. The question of independence can be misinterpreted as implying a somewhat distant, neutral role. A proper role should be one of informed critique and appropriate support.

Contrary to popular opinion, there is no distinction in law, or in role, between an executive and a non-executive board member. All board roles are non-executive; their responsibilities are for the overall well being and sustainability of the company, not to implement policies and strategies directly. If a board member additionally holds executive responsibilities, this does not absolve him or her from full board responsibilities. Experienced board adviser and author on governance Bob Garratt advises that executives who are also board directors have separate contracts. A job title with the term director should, in law in most jurisdictions, only be given to those individuals who are registered as directors with the relevant authorizing body: "You are either a registered director or you are not, from the legal viewpoint … Most people assume that the words 'managing' and 'directing' are synonymous. They are not" (Garratt, 2017).

It has followed from this that induction, preparation and training for board roles is often inadequate, although there is a growing number of business schools offering programmes for board roles, and some companies carry out reviews of board capability. Some business-owning families devote considerable resources to preparing the next generation for owner-governor roles, in the likelihood that senior executive positions will go to non-family candidates. The much-discussed "director's dilemma" refers to the apparently conflicting roles of providing support and resources to the executive team on the one hand, and also holding it to account. Arguably, however, while there can be tension between the roles, they are not mutually incompatible. Providing honest critiques of the strategies and conduct of the executive, and encouraging robust, challenging debate, is a form of support. Where a company has collapsed completely, typically the board has failed in both areas of responsibility. They may have failed to support a promising strategy to deal with a disruptive competitor, or been complacent about the dangers of a high-risk strategy. The common weakness is inadequate in-depth discussion about strategic risks and opportunities, by board members ill-prepared for their responsibilities.

11.5 Followership

All stakeholders and employees will have a fine-tuned sense, almost an instinct, about whether they can trust a governing body and the overall leadership of an organization. Trust covers sensitive issues such as whether one feels one will be treated fairly and whether bills and salaries will be paid. It also encompasses a sense of confidence on matters such as probity, environmental responsibility or wise investment. One can detect warning signals that something is not right in an institution where some weaknesses or malpractices are being covered up. These can also be picked up in a situation where the leader is not suited for the situation, and is not handling the major challenges and decisions facing him or her. A board is responsible for monitoring and maintaining trust. It is not a strategy as such, it is more a discipline, but it is one of central importance.

There is always both an individual and a group dynamic. If there are serious concerns about the top leader, and he or she is losing trust, the board will have to be aware and respond. But this has to be more than a focus on the individual, as a sole focus on the individual risks scapegoating (see Chapter 5). There will be group dynamics, there will be individual ambitions. Board members will need to inquire whether the concerns about the top leader are genuine or are rumors spread by rivals for the most senior role. If the board is passive and ineffective, it raises the risk of failed successions and the erosion of trust.

If there are weaknesses by the board in honouring this duty of care, there will be recurring worries, symptoms of anxiety and other emotions in the group/organization. Such concerns are likely to rise to the surface during a succession, and the more so if a succession fails. Of course, the appetite for risk varies by organization, as well as by individual. A leader or a stakeholder group might be able to persuade themselves and employees that adventure and short-term profits will create enough reward to warrant a risk to safety, but in such cases one is often dealing with a finite project rather than a long-lasting institution. And in such work environments there will be some members who experience a feeling of loss, and will have different degrees of mourning, with many wishing to move on to something new.

Practice Summary

All humans have a basic need for connection and safety, at least at some level. Tolerance for risk varies by individual, but there is always a ceiling, even for the most adventurous. The yearning and need for trust, therefore, are fundamental. It is often observed that trust can take years to build, but only a few moments to destroy – for example by a single but major act of betrayal of promises. This occurs because the act not only breaches the rules of engagement but gives a signal that the communication upon which trust had been built may have been dishonest all the way along. So the collapse of trust can be dramatic and complete.

Ultimately, even in the more adventurous organizations, the board cannot escape its responsibilities. Appetite for risk is one of the principles that a governing body has to establish, with a clear understanding of the impact as well as the likelihood of adverse outcomes, and contingency plans that suit. A board cannot negotiate away its fundamental duties, one of which is establishing and maintaining trust. No one benefits from institutional failure.

References

Costa, A. C., Fulmer, C. A., & Anderson, N. R. (2018). Trust in work teams: An integrative review, multilevel model, and future directions. *Journal of Organizational Behavior*, 39(2), 169–184.

Fulmer, C. A., & Gelfand, M. J. (2012). At what level (and in whom) we trust: Trust across multiple organizational levels. *Journal of Management*, 38(4), 1167–1230.

Garratt, B. (2017). *Stop the Rot*. Routledge.

Kramer, R. M. (1999). Trust and distrust in organizations: Emerging perspectives, enduring questions. *Annual Review of Psychology, 50*, 569–598.

12

THE SOCIAL AND PSYCHODYNAMIC IN SUCCESSIONS

The field of leadership has developed within different academic fields that inform how organizations, and groups, can be led the best. I explore, from a focus on a concrete phenomenon, how succession creates leadership. To give phenomena full justice I have used different strands of research but with an overall use of sociological and psychological perspectives. Since successions happen differently across cultures and institutions the mindset of seeing succession as a mechanism that is part of evolving organizations was important. It is an unavoidable part of social structures that aims to be more than a project. It will appear or be triggered with or without a strategic intent. But the space such a mechanism opens up with regards to strategic thinking is the key and crucial part of a succession. As mentioned throughout, succession has a high degree of complexity and rarely can rules and guidelines be used generally. Successions are unpredictable in nature and important for the group and its survival. Hence each succession has to be approached with care and addressed with the possibility of using new thinking and ingenuity.

The external reality of the group and external to the group is what we perceive and learn about and in between the needs and the external reality is our frontal cortex and its capacity to develop strategy and plans. The complexity is such that one has to define the tasks that one needs to set aside time to deliberate, discuss and take conscious decisions about. At this point the tasks or strategic challenges, seven different categories, will interact and thereby a best practice as a result of any combination of them is not possible to pin down. Furthermore, the emotional and group dynamic must also be considered. Being conscious or rational here means addressing the realm of irrationality. As such a to do list is not enough.

12.1 The How and Why Questions

The How Question in Succession

Leadership and management constitute a field that builds on psychology and sociological theory. Economics, law and social anthropology have also contributed with perspectives such as strategy, social contracts and cultural perspectives. Succession cannot, from a practice point of view, be fully understood with the use of any such academic field. Each field has significant contributions, but on its own is insufficient. In particular, as argued in this book, it is necessary to integrate perspectives from governance theory that often are bounded in legal theory as well as management theory informed by sociology and psychology.

Throughout the book I have drawn on sociology to describe roles in transition, and role histories as windows into how the dynamics of succession change top leadership roles over time. Sociological lenses allowed for pinpointing how institutional logics and succession systems differ. It inspired the idea of commissioning a classicist to draw on the study of ancient Rome and Greece, where much of Western cultural heritage originates, to look at succession as social systems. I have also relied, as my main academic background is in psychology, on psychological perspectives. In this chapter I will discusses more in depth the dynamics that can obstruct strategy formulation in successions. It builds on the chapters on group dynamics and individual emotions (Chapters 4 and 5). I also present, briefly and admittedly without giving the complex subject full justice, some of the latest findings in affective neuroscience that are of relevance. Findings from neuroscience on feelings and emotional needs also offer insights into features such as acceptance of sadness, lust, the need for safety and playfulness.

The Why behind the How

Sociology has explanatory power, through describing differences between practices in a society and comparison with others. It also reflects templates we internalize in our mind as scripts to follow for actions – these are often taken for granted as natural. They also have an emotional significance. A loss of a script or a challenge to one's social identity, and self image or ego, can lead to a loss process and, to different degrees for different individuals, a possible curiosity for a (ad)venture in new paths, new roles and social identities. Our work and social identities are partly scripted by cultural norms such as what one does and how we are assigned roles within a couple over a life span and long marriage. These scripts are, due to several reasons, radically changing. Roles are, with social changes in gender, family life and life stages, less rigid and scripted so one can no longer safely predict future trajectories. When one experiences losses, or changes to what would be a reasonable expectation, one has to acknowledge the loss and move on with new curiosity, experimentation and finding new safe spaces.

Understanding the psychological aspect as implication and intertwined with the social domain is crucial. It is a dimension often ignored in governance literature, but the emotional, or irrational and non-strategic domain, enables the exploration of why one designs governance in the first place. Issue of trust, the corruptive influence of power on the mind, the maneuvering through conflicts, balancing self-interests with the interests of the group and organization are all affected by human drive. There are ways one is influenced by internalized scripts and cognitive process influence our thinking and strategy. But, at the core are human needs and drives and how one takes up the challenge to lead or follow so as to meet the needs of oneself and others. As such one strategic capacity, located in the frontal cortex of the brain, is the intermediate area of negotiating and strategizing, the part of the brain that works out how to navigate the external reality and its demands in order to meet its needs. The implication of affective neuroscience will be briefly presented in the first section. Box 12.1 is dedicated specifically, without wearing out this drive, the difficulty with lust and trust in the workplace. The rest of this chapter explores how men and women can become destructive and vicariously use others to gain power. I explore the work hazard of CEOs, again relevant for both sexes, narcissism and hubris and lastly explore how tolerance of creative tension is important.

Human affects and feelings constitute much more complex drives, what is aversive and motivating, for behaviour than the more general punishments or rewards that are the basic assumption within traditional behavioural economics. New research findings, enabled by new instrumentation that can detect brain activity, has led to findings on human drive and feelings, or emotions, that have implications for leadership and followership. Affective neuroscience also confirms, revises or debunks assorted ideas in traditional psychoanalytic theory that now often are taken for granted in the leadership field and more generally.

12.2 Always Switched On: Feelings and Emotions

Many invest ambitions and hope into their work – far beyond only having a salary so as to be able to provide for one's physical needs. it is at the most senior levels, where the stakes involved in appointments and decisions are high, that some of the most dramatic psychological dramas occur, for example Bill Gross's exit process from Pimco (see Chapter 5). Powerful emotions can become destructive, and this risk is hugely increased where there is weak governance, for example resulting in hubris. Humans never reach nirvana; we always have unmet needs. Feelings are the means of registering these needs. There isn't any point at which they are switched off, and there isn't any context in which they don't matter.

Over the last ten years new research on the biological basis for human needs and drive has consolidated as a separate field within psychology. Affective neuroscience combines neuroscience with psychoanalytic ideas on drive and needs, or emotions, and has become a hard science that is quantitative and based on experiments, that give confirmation and refute ideas within psychoanalytic theory. Psychology has gone through several trends over the last 40–50 years where behaviourism and later cognitive psychology dominated. Each has contributed with important findings. The difficulty with capturing feelings and emotions with hard science, that is quantitative research, has led it to be ignored as a legitimate research focus and occasionally leading the field to argue that emotions and feelings do not exist as biological parts of the brain or without specific valence in their own right. The latter would be a social construction perspective that implies that our interpretation based on reading our social context is what gives us a notion that we are scared, sad, happy or any other interpretation of a feeling. Tell that to a baby of one year old with a furious face and who cries to protest the loss of a caregiver going out of the room when the baby wanted something specific. Or the laughter one can trigger with the same baby in the game of peekaboo over the rim of the pram.

Freud suggested the concept of the Id, our sexual needs as lust and rage, were the emotional needs we were born with in addition to physical needs. These were instinctual and in our young years, during our upbringing, would become censored and therefore relegated to the unconscious. Lust and rage were the main drives that would, according to traditional psychoanalytic theory, be sublimated into creative work or, less successfully, could become the cause of neuroses or serious dysfunctions. The domain of work and cultural activities would be seen as healthy sublimation, a creative outlet, for the otherwise unconscious and repressed lustful and destructive or aggressive feelings. Within in this old Freudian worldview lust was paramount for all other activities and if one struggled in that domain, such as in work, it was due to how the sublimation did not work and one was neurotic, repeating old non-functional ways to meet sexual needs or to vent one's aggression and rage.

To explain a further complication in the relationship between genders, the different roles and the relationship to one's internal and external authority, Freud used the Oedipus complex. He also used it to explain why he thought lust and anger were rendered unconscious. In 1922 he wrote about group dynamics and group formation. He regarded a group as coming together out of a sense of common fate, collaboration and cohesion. These aspects make a group converge so as to develop activities that sustain it beyond the actual tasks at hand. Membership also means that some individual needs may need to be set aside, or diminished by agreement, giving priority to the goals of the group. This can result in individuals displaying constructive competition or destructive rivalry, complicating the internal dynamics.

Affective neuroscience has found we are born with at least seven biological primary processes and hence adding five to the two Freud suggested. These needs, such as a need for safety, playfulness and care, would not be sublimations of a repressed lust or rage as Freud would have seen it. Crucially, the latest understanding of unconsciousness is that these needs and emotions are not in themselves unconscious. The Oedipus explanation is not seen as relevant in suggesting that sexual and aggressive instincts/needs have to become unconscious. Rather, all these instincts and needs, Id, are part of our consciousness. We often can report and describe them. What is unconscious are the strategies and scripts developed through out experiences, often failed attempts, to meet those needs. The Ego constitutes these correct or incorrect replications and predictions and is the source of unconscious strategies and memories. These primary biological and hard wired needs are the source, through learning and experience, for more complex and secondary processes of emotions such as trust, guilt, envy, empathy and gratitude. The leading neuropsychologist and psychoanalyst Mark Solms describes the fundamental change with affective neuroscience (*from a private conversation*):

> Feelings announce needs. They can be basic needs, like feeling thirsty, hungry. Those are all feelings but not emotions. That's a fundamental starting point. The social feelings announce how you're doing in relation to your needs; the further away you are, the worse it feels. This is all tied to the basic need: the need to survive. This applies to all feelings, including emotional feelings. Emotional feelings – sadness, panic-grief, rage, lust as wanting and liking, fun in playfulness, the excitement of curiosity – are all emotional feelings that are the experience of biological circuits in the mid-brain. They are all hard wired in the mid-brain, not in our cortex.

There is no point in time at which human feelings are absent, or switched off, or non-relevant to the way in which we behave and perform in groups. The needs for lust, playfulness that also establishes social systems, exploration and curiosity in hunting for "something", to bond so as to feel safe, to take care of, fearfulness so as to be on guard and rage so as to be able to protect ourselves are all triggered in assorted circumstances. They are contradictory and may, in any situation, force us to make choices that can be difficult. Over time we also learn to integrate and align them. The more that is at stake – work security, career, prospects of a prestigious new job – the more they are triggered and the more difficult it is to make choices that reflect emotional maturity. This emotional maturity, developed over one's life, guides one in how to act so as to have realistic strategies for meeting one's needs. It also enables one to sacrifice or postpone one need for another, or align them so as to create innovative solutions.

12.3 Lust in the Workplace

Playfulness and the social group, how people use play to create social systems and innovations, are dynamics that often require a leader to uphold the rules. There are boundaries and choices to be made, just as there are in regards to attraction and lust. Affective neuroscience is used as a platform to delve into some of the more complex themes that are relevant in succession dynamics. Gender is one of these. With the increased influence of feminism, and more professional women at senior levels, our thinking about the workplace has to change. As noted in Chapter 6 we have logics on leadership, and unconscious biases, that inhibit us from thinking of leadership of women in a neutral way. Stories on leadership, especially legends and other historical material, as highlighted in some of the case studies in this book, gravitate towards male models and scripts.

Over the course of our history women have rarely been in power and often depicted as, and have been, victims. It would be beyond the scope of this book to give a comprehensive analysis of gender in the workplace. I will focus on lust and trust in the workplace where men's and women's wants and desires are asymmetrical and complicated. I bear in mind that both men and women flirt and look for sex at work. The difference between a flirt and a sexual relationship is in the feeling, a flirt is an "as if" and can be innocent as one is curious and playing with the idea of an encounter or having a liking for someone. If the difference between as if as playfulness and as a strategy for meeting sexual needs can not be upheld one is ill advised to flirt. To enter into a sexual relationship in a work place is to act out a strategy of wanting to meet sexual needs, not keeping it as a playful as if, and will always corrupt decision making processes and the legitimacy of one's role and work.

We seem to have some ideas that sexual attraction in the workplace has led women to fail in career progression or success, or has been one of the strategies for success. To what extent sexual dynamics influenced the different trajectories cannot be clarified in a scientific way. Nor is the full implication of how men have sanctioned women who have not succumbed to a seduction. Certainly these complex dynamics have affected women's careers, experiences of work and how they would dare to aspire for roles they were qualified for.

But I think it is naïve to ignore how attractive power is in getting others', both men's and women's, attention. Men just have a more limited set of options, and many male rituals safeguard how they can socialize in social settings where women don't have access. That acknowledged dynamic of power, attraction and the unsymmetrical relationship between the wanting of power and sex could make the relationship between anyone, regardless of gender and sexual orientation, a complex domain to manoeuvre in. It is an old theme (see Box 12.1) written about by Ovid, year 8 BC, inspiring Bernini in 1622 and, with the accusations raised against Harvey Weinstein in 2018, for the first time in history it is being broadly discussed and addressed.

BOX 12.1 LUST AND TRUST – DAPHNE AND APOLLO

By Agnes Wilhelmsen

Daphne and Apollo, in Ovid's *Metamorphoses*, Book 1, written in 8 AD, inspired the sculptor Bernini in 1622. The fable resonates with the power of seduction, and also with abuse of power. In the year 2018 a scandal, and possible court cases, implicates the movie mogul Harvey Weinstein. He is facing several accusations of sexual assault from actresses whose careers could have been affected by his granting or withdrawal of favour. In *Metamorphoses* Ovid captures, as does Bernini, the allure of semigods, the chase and self-representation after such sexual assault. Below is an imagined satirical response to the drama.

The Trial

Judge: Any allegation of non-consensual sex is unequivocally denied by Apollo. Apollo has further confirmed that there were never any acts of retaliation against Daphne for refusing his advances.

Daphne (reminiscently): Those golden tumbling locks I had heard so much about swaying gently around his neck, on the sides of his temples like torches of light. I had just escaped my dad's usual spiel about all the well-bred boys, bored by it, out on my usual hunt I recognized him, the archer Apollo.

He was known for his booming stride resplendent in all his gear. I gazed at him from afar, his smooth olive-skin glittering with speckled rays of sun beneath crowded thickets of flowering ash and truffle oak. The rumours were spreading ... that ever-young god had slain a mighty python and wished to garland his tender temples in his victory. I shivered a little at the thought... All morning I had spent thrilled in the chase for a deer... competing with the Delian twin. Enjoying the quiet in a moment of rest I suddenly noticed him – Apollo – looking back.

Excited, I tried to meet the mighty god's gaze. Only he wasn't looking at me. I followed his gaze... scanning the scene we both caught sight of a boy fumbling about with a bow, Cupid, and—

Apollo (interrupting righteously): He was not fumbling about! The impudent little boy pierced my heart with that golden-tipped arrow of his that kindles love. Up to the top of mount Parnassus he flies bringing back these wretched arrows and... *and* the bloody girl was shot too! But with a silver-tipped one that incites flight! We were both!!!

Judge: Sir! This is not permitted in my court! Proceed, Daphne.

Exhibit A:

Source: *Alamy*

Daphne: I looked back to Apollo... but he was right next to me. Startled but eager to meet him I went to shake his hand, which he grabbed greedily, yanking my whole body with it. I tried to shrug him off light-heartedly telling him "No, no, no," but he insisted,. We both moved, one in hope the other in fear...

Then he tried to get more physical, sort of chasing me around. I couldn't believe it. At this point I was like, what the fuck!

Apollo (interrupting again): I am the son of Zeus! My arrow is exact but there is one whose is more – damn impudent boy – ah me!

Daphne (somewhat admiringly): I did think at the time about Apollo as a god ... a poet beyond compare, Phoebus the *bright*, master of the arts, "an icon in the entertainment industry" ... untouchable ... the son of Zeus ... I recollected those golden tumbling curls, that gleaming olive skin, dejected but then attracted. That hazy glow of honour that would follow him wherever he went ... it was still alluring to me.

Then he properly chased me, dick, balls and all ... he literally chased me.

Apollo: Look, I won't do it again. Don't ruin your friendship with me for five minutes.

Exhibit B:

Source: Alamy

Daphne: Just ... move forward, I urged myself on as I sped across the terrain, Apollo's pleas of love echoing all around me, his voice like a sweetly-sounding lyre: "Come on. Please. I'm right behind you. I want to touch your tits. Kiss you a little." The place grew wilder ... I skirted around a lofty oak but was blocked by a fallen silver fir. ... Then he pushed me and rammed me up against the oak's trunk and started fumbling at my gown.

Being up close to him made me realize how big and fat Apollo really was. I ducked, dived and ultimately got out of there without getting slobbered over. Sprinting, I felt my heart was really racing. I was in a fight-or-flight mode. Frantic in flight I suddenly remembered the river my father would sit by in the afternoon fishing... (*dreamily*) I would sometimes join him, exhausted after my morning hunt I would give my father whatever I had caught and rest beside him ... dozing off to the sweet scurry of water hurrying down the river-bank...

Judge: Where is this going, Daphne?

Daphne (with difficulty): With all my heart I had hoped he would be there. I felt my chin soar back as Apollo yanked my hair, mouth gaping, the pressure on my throat immense under the weight of the god.

It grew very quiet and he whispered, "This is how things work in Hollywood."

Apollo (in strained hexameter): "I who pursue thee am no enemy. Oh stay! Doves on fluttering wing flee from the eagle; creature flees its foes. But love is the cause of my pursuit. Ah me..."

Judge: Apollo!

Daphne: ... I struggled but I had very little strength left in me. Frozen with fear a "deep languor took hold of my limbs". I felt like I was drowning under the weight of Apollo into the moist earth, my feet no longer swift found themselves among roots. My skin lost its heat and like smooth bark, enveloped me in a shroud of thin frost. And Apollo grabs me... he holds me by the back of the neck, grabbing and holding tightly to the back of my arm. The next thing I know, he's pressing against me...

Exhibit C:

Source: *Alamy*

... no, no, no... the words disappear in my thoughts.
Apollo (bursting in like a raging bull): I will kill you, don't think I can't.
Daphne: There I lay still like a dead person... it was the single most damaging thing that's happened in my life.

12.4 Volumnia and Kingmakers at Work

It is also well acknowledged that men have been, throughout history, in positions of power and at high levels within organizations. No serious thinker or practitioner would dispute this. Some might be claiming that men are by nature supposed to be dominant and women submissive, but that is not supported by any science or indeed by any modern ideology. This is an old theme and it has been much explored and debated. Feminism has been highly successful even though many don't want to call themselves a feminist. In many of the family cases researched for this book it was a married couple founding the firm, with the wife taking a leading role. If one examines family dynamics, the influence of women has been perhaps even more hidden than conventionally understood. They have certainly not been without influence. Throughout history women of intelligence have had power, but not necessarily executive discretion – that is influence given in a negotiated and formal way. Effective authority – the ability to convey influence based on achievements, talent and understanding – is another matter than power. To argue that women have always wielded power is to acknowledge that it might not have been seen as legitimate – they took it and used it.

Executive discretion and authority are less ambiguous terms than power. They can be identified and discussed in a good succession process. They are open for scrutiny, and one is accountable to someone, or it may be based on performance. Arguing that women always have had power is therefore a trap – it deflects from the fact that women have not been entitled to powerful roles unless through men. Power is a fluid capability to have – it can be taken away and it can constantly shift; it often builds on lack of accountability and may create resentment. Eleanor of Aquitaine, for example, was de facto monarch of England and large parts of France for periods in the late 12th Century, without being formally crowned. Through their husbands and sons, many resourceful women have indirectly wielded significant executive power.

In many ways, even though it is not full equality, feminism has been radically successful and changed society and working life. Yes, it is frustrating that it goes slowly. On the basic and important issues raised by feminists, apart form abortion, few would argue a regression of those rights. With this as context it is important to also know how women, in work and social life, can use power in a subtle way. It is also not exclusive to a woman in a relationship with a man but can be used by anyone claiming to be the enabler of someone else. The following narrative captured an aspect of how one can be the victim of frustrated female ambitions. Shakespeare captured this in the character Volumnia, mother of a Roman hero Coriolanus. While it is here seen a gendered context, and I will keep it as such in the narrative, there is an aspect of how one can, as someone without legitimacy at the formal level, use power in a destructive way. With this I hope to represent emotional, often unconscious, dynamics that can influence succession dynamics in significant but subtle ways. Not only are top leaders and CEOs supported on the way up to the top by family, colleagues and friends, there might also be someone designating themselves into becoming, or being, the kingmaker.

At the centre of the play *Coriolanus* is a relationship not often explored by Shakespeare: a powerful mother and the son she has shaped in her image. Volumnia is a fierce woman, noble by birth, clever and an excellent strategist, more so than Coriolanus, the general and leader in the play. Had she been able to join the Roman army, as her late husband and inevitably her son had, she would have done so. Instead, she channels her ambition, pride and decisiveness into her son. Through mentoring Coriolanus she shapes him as soldier, victorious commander but ultimately becomes his nemesis and the cause of his downfall and death. She then emerges as the de facto ruler. It is not a play that is often staged, but Ralph Fiennes and Vanessa Redgrave take on these two roles in a film, directed by Fiennes in 2011.

In a psychodynamic understanding, the mother in this drama is acting out her own wish and ambition for power. She was, in raising and later mentoring her son, nurturing her own ambitions, projected onto him. He becomes a fierce and successful general but lacks her capacity for strategy and becomes a bit lost. Volumnia identifies with his ambitions and her lexicon is of the warrior male, terms of conquest, power and military glory. She is described as harbouring the value of honour and valour above life – for example, she is delighted when she receives the news that her son has been wounded in battle. She has no patience or empathy with her daughter-in-law, the more conventionally feminine Virgilia, representing vulnerability in the play. Volumnia guides Coriolanus in how to win people over but is increasingly disappointed and frustrated. Coriolanus is left withering between alliances with the enemy and his own group and is killed in no man's land. Volumnia arises to become the leader of the state. She tragically has risen to what he, and she, aimed for while she also dooms him to death at the hands of the enemy.

It is relevant in many ways for organizations to understand how men and women, through frustration or lack of opportunity, might use others as tools for their own need for power. The kingmaker is a self-designated, or real, role but the relationship will always be complex and at best should only be one of gratitude, without any debt, for the opportunity of having being mentored or being the mentor. The notion of Volumnia at work also captures an elite preservation strategy. At a social level and elite level high-status parents use substantial resources and time on coaching, providing tutors and mentoring for their children to secure them a place in the right nurseries, prestigious schools and the best universities. In extreme cases it leads to parents cheating on behalf of their children. This phenomenon of elite parenting is included in a wider critique of meritocracy in *The Meritocracy Trap*, by Daniel Markovits (2019). Overall we need diverse elites and access to top leadership positions and leadership teams. The offspring and children are, due to their parent's narcissism and projection of their own needs onto the child, left wandering aimlessly in a no man's land. The psychoanalyst Winnicott coined the term of the "False Self", a sense of being a bit empty, lost in not knowing one's own desires to capture how we, when being filled with others' desires and ambitions, are trying to find our own way (Winnicott, 1996). In close relationship and between the board and CEO or a chair and CEO, such frustration and ambition can cripple one as leader with a sense of their own drive and ambition. Even if one can comply with a growth and conventional strategy the capability to create innovative strategy might be lost.

12.5 The CEO Work Hazards: Narcissism and Hubris

Big egos and narcissistic tendencies constitute a familiar theme in human history, especially business and politics, with outspoken, supposedly high-achieving characters such as Donald Trump. The personality type is also prominent in fiction, for example dramas on film and TV that feature flamboyant leaders with sprawling business empires and complicated love lives, both of which provoke intense rivalries and jealousies. As discussed in Chapter 5, this is a complex and eventually a destructive dynamic. Some leaders with narcissistic tendencies can be effective; moreover, a healthy self-regard and good confidence levels are attributes.

Where narcissism becomes a disorder is where an individual self-aggrandizes to the point of being delusional; another symptom is an extreme form of splitting – dividing the world into others (bad) and one-self (good). Such individuals exhibit self-satisfaction, which is a need to be admired without reciprocity, a need to be loved and a high degree of self-love without capacity for genuine love for others. Their apparent affection for others is predominantly a means of using people for their own ends. Some may be highly effective in this, exhibiting powerful charm, but in a powerful position the "disease" of narcissism will only get worse and increase delusional thinking. Increasingly they will possess a sense of being unbeatable or hubristic, creating high risks for a company and the decision-making process. Behind the narcissistic defense that seeks, and demands, attention and praise there is a dark and fragile area of vulnerabilities and insecurities. These concepts and theories are well developed within mainstream psychological and psychoanalytic theory as well as leadership theory.

Narcissism would appear to be an individualistic trait but, as with all other aspects of psychodynamics, it is also a group phenomenon. Importantly, narcissism can often develop to destructive levels after a leader has success, or gets a powerful role and position in a group. They can be prone to appointing sycophants, including to senior roles, thus weakening leadership, as the emphasis is on personal power and prestige rather than effectiveness. The sycophant aspect is often ignored but is a part of group dynamics, with over-idealization of a leader. The group aspect of narcissism is often overlooked but is a very strong feature in the 2,500-year-old fable of the Greek god Narcissus that inspired Freud to describe and write about narcissism. He was not the first one to do so and the myth's significance has always denoted, as it does now, how a person can get lost in love with themselves but also what it does with the group, in the myth represented by Echo (see Box 12.2).

BOX 12.2 BEFORE NARCISSUS WAS ECHO

By Agnes Wilhelmsen

In Ovid's *Metamorphoses*, Echo is a nymph who is cursed by Juno for her relentless chattering, which diverts Juno's attention away from the philandering escapades of her husband, Jupiter. Now Echo can only speak when spoken to and manages only to utter the last few words of what is said. She meets Narcissus when they both are out wandering. Narcissus is outstandingly beautiful. As the myth goes Echo catches sight of Narcissus and falls in love with him. When Narcissus loses his other companions, he calls out "Is there anybody here?" to which Echo repeats "Here!". Echo is unable to vocalize her passion for Narcissus but she makes use of her voice the best she can. Even when Narcissus scornfully rejects Echo she manages to express her desire:

"Away with these embraces! I would die before I would have you touch me!"
Her only answer was: "I would have you touch me!"

(Innes, 1995)

Echo in shame hides and wastes away in death. Her bones, they say, turned to stone and only her voice and the echo remains. In this place the echo mournfully repeats Narcissus' own lament whose realization of his beauty renders him incapable of parting with his reflection.

His last words as he gazed into the familiar waters:

"Woe is me for the boy I loved in vain!"
And from the stones comes the echo of the last same words.

(Innes, 1995)

A prophet predicts that Narcissus will live long if he does "not come to know himself" and from a young age Narcissus bears "a pride so unyielding ... no one dared touch him." (Innes, 1995) Narcissus' beauty attracts both girls and boys, rendering him a somewhat androgynous figure. Narcissus and Echo are fluid figures and their dynamic transcends binary gender relations.

Echo metamorphoses into a voice after her death, which eternally commemorates her futile and lost infatuation and love. This is a powerful metamorphosis in light of the consistent rejection her agency undergoes and showcases the sycophantic force: one who loses the ability to speak freely and is bound to repeat only what they hear. The narcissist is a powerful figure based on some material value (in this case physical beauty), whose encounter with the world is eschewed by a continual aggrandizement of their material value. With Narcissus it is ambiguous as he becomes a victim of his beauty but by the end a true narcissist and his own perpetuator.

A narcissistic leader might not accept critique or feedback unless it is redefined as a learning process. They rarely seek therapy and if they do it is because they are forced into the situation by a partner or have failed in a post in an obvious way. Rarely do they see their internal sense of vulnerability and inferiority as the origin of their problem. Often they will use the defense of splitting, one of the most primitive defense mechanisms, and divide the world into good and bad people. This is a mechanism that mitigates the emotional pain they would have were they to address their sense of inferiority. The board can also provide such a learning forum for a CEO, and in this way accept a certain degree of narcissism. Furthermore, boards are the type of social structure that makes narcissistic leaders accountable and counteracts narcissistic development. In a coaching process one can with some astute and skillful coaching, at least for a while, help narcissistic leaders hold onto their feelings of and thoughts about their vulnerabilities and sense of inferiority. Often one has to contract with such leaders that it is a learning process directed forwards without addressing the sense of inferiority directly. It might be as good as it gets and while one can arrest the development, maybe create some improvement, one is then helping others to protect themselves and any board to regain a role of accurately monitoring and maintaining accountability.

Practice Summary

Throughout the book I have described and gone into detail of how any group, and a governing body, can use the succession in a strategic way and thereby safeguard the long-term survival of the organization while managing destructive processes. The following is five discussion points so as to initiate a thorough process, and to create some process goals, for succession processes.

1. Governing role(s). Acknowledge the destructive potential and threats with a review of procedure and succession system. The succession process is a transition so as to equip organizational development and learning, enabling it better to confront new challenges and a changed context. It is necessary to analyse if challenges calling for renewal are best met with a succession or incubation process or with both processes in sequence or parallel.
2. Ownership evolution. Within private ownership, entrepreneurship, next generation owner and new leadership dynamics there are, in successions, more strategic and emotional complexities. Hence there are also more possibilities for innovation in the succession process. Tension can be converted to creative tension. It helps to redefine the goal as being one of enhancing autonomy and creative opportunities, rather than the zero-sum concept of winners and losers.
3. Strategy tool. To present the implications for practitioners it is necessary to have a focus on how succession and strategy demand an

integrated contribution. The Succession Strategy Wheel is such an initiative. It builds on the research cases, client cases, experiences of chairs of boards gathered through interview and earlier research.

4. Taking emotions and group dynamics seriously. The emotions and drive involved in succession will always be powerful. Emotional elements can include ambition, ego, rivalry and loss, but they do not necessarily have a destructive impact. Awareness and insight are necessary for the board, the leader exiting the role and the successor in preparing for and for the entry into the role.

5. Frames. Careful use of vocabulary can be helpful for advisers moving boards and other teams away from the lexicon of conflict. Concepts such as authority, autonomy and role can defuse concepts that are laden with emotion and association such as power, ambition or individual. Furthermore, they refer to a process, rather than a state, a position or something to have or to fear. A process of developing autonomy, which incorporates the concepts of innovation and negotiation, opens up conversations that are less value-laden, and less likely to trigger individual or group resistance.

References

Innes, M. M. (1995). *The metamorphoses of Ovid* (tr.). Penguin Books.

Markovits, D. (2019). *The meritocracy trap: How America's foundational myth feeds inequality, dismantles the middle class, and devours the elite.* Penguin Press.

Winnicott, D. W. (1996). Ego distortion in terms of true and false self. In V. Richards (Ed.), *The person who is me: Contemporary perspectives on the true and false* (pp. 7–22). Routledge.

INDEX